Jacaré Assu

Brazilian Colonization, from an European point of view

Jacaré Assu

Brazilian Colonization, from an European point of view

ISBN/EAN: 9783743349551

Manufactured in Europe, USA, Canada, Australia, Japa

Cover: Foto ©ninafisch / pixelio.de

Manufactured and distributed by brebook publishing software (www.brebook.com)

Jacaré Assu

Brazilian Colonization, from an European point of view

BRAZILIAN COLONIZATION,

FROM AN EUROPEAN POINT OF VIEW.

BY

JACARÉ ASSU.

LONDON:
EDWARD STANFORD, 6 & 7, CHARING CROSS, S.W.

1873.

PREFACE.

THE facts on which the following reflections on colonization in Brazil are grounded, have been derived from personal experience, intercourse, and observation; from the published treatises of Senhor Tavares Bastos, and of the German Consul, Hermann Haupt, members of a patriotic Brazilian society for the encouragement of emigration; from the work of Herr von Tschudi, formerly Swiss Minister in Brazil, and from other less important sources.

BRAZILIAN COLONIZATION.

Some people say that it is better to crimp cod-fish, and that the best way to kill a calf is by bleeding it to death.

Some people, again, think emigration of Englishmen to Brazil advisable. It is easy enough to understand these assertions, and many similar ones, and yet to hold a diametrically opposite opinion. The fact is, so much depends on the point of view. In the following lines I propose to take my stand rather with the cod-fish, calves, and colonists, than with gourmands and colonization agents. Brazil has been contemplated so often from the rosy point of view; people paid and unpaid have at various times been so fulsomely mendacious on her account; placards, newspapers, guide-books, and itineraries, have contained such startling paragraphs—often under the hand of those who ought to have known better—about the marvellous fertility of the empire and the exceptional advantages it offers, that a little sober truth becomes more than ever necessary. And this is especially the case at a moment when the demand for white labour consequent on the Slavery Abolition Bill, to say nothing of particular interests, has given a new stimulus to the emigrant trade. For it is with emigrating as it is with crimping cod-fish and bleeding calves—few constitutions will stand a repetition of the process. To be once either crimped or emigrated is enough, or more than enough, for one lifetime. "Emigrated"—yes, that is the rub. If the advantages of Brazil, its balmy climate, its deep soil, its mineral wealth, its warm reception of emigrants, its rigid adherence to contracts, its sound institutions, and the affinities of its people for things and minds Teutonic, were left to spread their light by the radiating force of truth alone; if the importation of whites was restricted to facilitating the transit and establishment of those who followed that natural attraction which the means of wealth and happiness necessarily exercises upon the poor and miserable—without official meddling, subsidizing, or puffing—if these were the conditions of the movement, then there would, indeed, be nothing to say against it. But would it then ever take place at all? As far as regards the English agricultural labourer, I think we may answer, "never"; as it is, he is *emigrated*, contracted for at so much a head, caught like a fly by a pretty paper, tickled by hyperbolical expectations, hallucinated with visions of an earthly Paradise; and thus, addleheaded, dumb-cattle like, reliant on others, helpless and exacting, he is shipped off to the Eldorado to be *sold*.

The object of the Brazilian is perfectly plain and

comprehensible. He wants work done, and has himself an innate personal aversion to doing it. As the country develops and old races die, degenerate, or adopt the same view of labour as himself, he is compelled to seek fresh blood and sinew. It is important to him that they should be of the best suitable and available quality. Accustomed, in a sense shockingly literal, to look on labour, that is man, as a commodity, the question of how he gets it, is one about which he is not likely to be over-scrupulous. How he has hitherto got it is well known. Africans were imported, Aborigines were ransomed—that is, bought or stolen. Even now the "captains of Indians"* illegally constrain the freedom of the uncivilized natives, as the monstrous law of contract for services legally does the unwary immigrant. Of this unscrupulousness in supplying a sudden demand for human beings, the recruiting for the last war gave painful instances. It was not always easy to distinguish a "voluntario da patria" rallying to the standard from the return of a runaway slave. That the action of the Brazilian emigration agents has at times been scarcely more scrupulous than that of the recruiting officer, the fate of the emigrant scarcely more enviable than that of the recruit, has been occasionally too manifest to European eyes.

* Certain officials on the borders of civilization specially concerned with the care of the Indians.

Portuguese still emigrate by thousands to the land discovered by their forefathers; bronzed sons of the volcanic islands, or of the scarcely less burning plains of Lusitania, good workers, good Catholics, allied in blood and habits, what can be the objection to them? A very simple one; they will not stop. Many at least go back by the way that they came, bearing with them the spoil of the tropics. Pedro Chumbo will venture capital or strength under the Southern cross, but, in a great majority of cases, it is only that he may some day build his palace on the hills of the Tagus or purchase a few acres of his native volcano. The Frenchman is no colonist, the Spaniard and Italian merely peddle in trade or go elsewhere.

With an exaggerated notion of the misery of northern Europe and an erroneous one of the tendency of poverty to moderate men's exigencies, the Brazilian looked to Alpine valleys and lands washed by foggy northern seas for the stuff he required. Doubly disappointed in the results, he coquetted a little with the Yankee and the Pole in times of their misfortune, and once in desperation with the Coolie, but only to return again to the old Boreal source.

From his own point of view, this is at any rate intelligible; but would it be equally so, that the Anglo-Saxon should, without once weighing the costs and profits, play blindly into his hands? There will always be boors enough tempted to go on board the gilded galley, as long as one lies in a British port. It is better to suggest caution beforehand than afterwards to raise the futile cry, "Que diable allaient-ils faire dans cette galère?"

Of all persons, why select for this most tentative experiment, the Anglo-Saxon, on whose wide choice of home-ruled domiciles the sun never goes down? Between Canada and the Cape, Vancouver's and the Falklands, New Zealand and the Himalayas, Belize and Pegu, one would have thought there was sufficient work cut out and elbow-room enough, in all conscience, for our surplus Islanders, without their flying laws, religion, rites, and mother-tongue, in the depths of a damp Sertaô.* Sons of an empire embracing one-third of the surface of the globe, with a million square miles in Asia, two millions and a half in Australia, and more than half a million in North America, what has that of the Southern cross to do with them? Between eternal ice and torrid glow, between the level of the condor and that of the cuckoo, between the chase of the walrus and that of the wombat, between the cultivation of orchella and that of the oil-palm, between the preparation of kelp or coffee, let them choose; but keep together!

Notwithstanding Messrs. Burton and Kingsley (curious collocation!), the Englishman does suffer in the tropics, and if, as the former implies, the steam-

* Jungles and backwoods of Brazil.

ing woods of the torrid zone are to be the habitation of the ideal man of the future, that man must be the Nigger, or at least more allied to the ape than we are. But if there are men who still have dreams of sitting under their own palm-trees, smoking their own fresh-plucked tobacco, have we not tropica' lands enough, without trying to graft blackthorn upon banana, the Saxon on Mulatto or Iberian? Is not Guiana equal to vast tracts in Brazil? Are there no western Indies waiting a second lease of life, almost a rediscovery?

What is it then that has from time to time drawn troops of our countrymen to the Southern Empire? Speculation? placards? or sound information? British interests or Brazilian?

Is it the experience of other nations and the fate of former colonies?

Here is a list of the colonies of the Empire, published by the "Sociedade International de Immigração," established for the purpose of advancing the cause of immigration, and brought down to 1866. Since then, a certain number of wealthy and intelligent Americans from the vanquished Southern States, and some most unsatisfactory consignments both from the States and from England, complete the list of Brazilian experiences of colonization at high pressure :—

EXPERIENCES OF OTHER COUNTRIES. 9

	Colonias.	Provincias.	Epocas de sua fundação.
1	Nova-Friburgo	Rio de Janeiro	1817
2	S. Leopoldo	Rio-Grande do Sul	1825
3	Tres-Forquilha	Rio-Grande do Sul	1826
4	S. Pedro de Alcantara das Torres ..	Rio-Grande do Sul	1826
5	S. Pedro de Alcantra	Santa Catharina	1828
6	Rio-Negro	Paraná	1828
7	Itajahy	Santa Catharina	1835
8	Petropolis	Rio de Janeiro	1846
9	Santa Isabel e Vargem-Grande	Santa Catharina	1845
10	Santa Isabel	Espirito-Santo	1847
11	Nossa Senhora da Piedade	Santa Catharina	1847
12	Santa-Cruz	Rio-Grande do Sul	1849
13	D. Pedro II.	Rio-Grande do Sul	1850
14	Monte-Bonito	Rio-Grande do Sul	1850
15	Rincão d'El-Rei	Rio-Grande do Sul	1850
16	Mundo-Novo	Rio-Grande do Sul	1850
17	Blumenau	Santa Catharina	1850
18	D. Theresa	Paraná	1850
19	D. Francisca	Santa Catharina	1851
20	Mucury ou Philadelphia	Espirito-Santo	1852
21	Colonias por parceria, em numero de 37, já mencionadas..	S. Paulo	1852
22	Santa Isabel	Maranhão	1853
23	Conventos	Rio-Grande do Sul	1854
24	Silva	Rio-Grande do Sul	1854
25	Superaguy	Paraná	1854
26	Nossa Senhora do O'	Pará	1855
27	Peçanha	Pará	1855
28	Silva	Pará	1855
29	Arapapchy	Maranhão	1855
30	Santa Isabel	Maranhão	1855
31	Santa Theresa	Maranhão	1855
32	Perucana	Maranhão	1855
33	Petropolis	Maranhão	1855
34	Independencia	Rio de Janeiro	1855
35	Santa Rosa	Rio de Janeiro	1855
36	Santa Justa	Rio de Janeiro	1855
37	Corôas	Rio de Janeiro	1855
38	Vallão do Veado	Rio de Janeiro	1855
39	Robillon	S. Paulo	1855
40	Santa Leopoldina	Espirito-Santo	1856
41	Rio-Novo	Espirito-Santo	1856
42	Transylvania	Espirito-Santo	1856
43	Mariante	Rio-Grande do Sul	1856
44	Estrella	Rio-Grande do Sul	1856
45	D. Affonso	Santa Catharina	1856
46	Leopoldina	Santa Catharina	1856
47	Sinimbú	Bahia	1857

Colonias.	Provincias.	Epocas de sua fundaçao.
48 S. Angelo	Rio-Grande do Sul	1857
49 Santa Maria da Soledade	Rio-Grande do Sul	1857
50 Nova Petropolis	Rio-Graude do Sul	1858
51 S. Lourenço	Rio-Grande do Sul	1858
52 Engenho-Novo	Bahia	1859
53 Rio-Pardo	Bahia	1860
54 S. Diogo	Piauhy	1860
55 D. Pedro II.	Rio de Janeiro	1860
56 Iguape	S. Paulo	1860
57 Cananéa	S. Paulo	1860
58 Assunguy	Paraná	1860
59 Theresopolis	Santa Catharina	1860
60 Itajahy	Santa Catharina	1860
61 Angelina	Santa Catharina	1860
62 S. Vicente de Paula	Piauhy	1861
63 Mont' Alverne	Rio-Grande do Sul	1862
64 Encruzilhada	Rio-Grande do Sul	1862
65 Empreza de Mme. Langendorf	Paraná	1865
66 Colonia allemã	Santa Catharina	1827
67 Colonia belga	Santa Catharina	1844

It is Switzerland that, in the colony of Nova Fribourgo, founded in 1818–1820, makes the first sad entry on this list.

Nova Fribourgo, with its broad, silent plaza; the white houses, backed by grey hills of noble form; the green, planted round with Araucarias and arborescent Bougainvillea; with its church and Camára, with its President and Vereadores, with its judges and delegados, with its police and national guard, the organized municipality exists at this day, and looks forward, by reason of its new railroad station, to a brilliant future; but of the Swiss who first broke ground there, a few scattered families in or round the town are the only representatives.

Five thousand volunteered in Bern, a part only of whom left Switzerland. Owing to delays and other circumstances, including fevers caught in Holland, but 2006 of these sailed from the ports of Rotterdam and Amsterdam; only 1682 reached the marshy foot of the Serra do Mar, in which deadly region it had pleased the Brazilian Government to fix their first temporary bivouac. Thirty-one died in the hospital of Macuco; of the thin remnant that reached the site of the colony, 146 followed in the course of a month, mostly from the effects of sufferings in the swamps below.*

The struggle with that kind of tropical luxuriance which grows by sunlight and water alone, and the attempt to conjure something better out of the decomposed granite, soon exhausted the lives or patience of the mass of the survivors, so that, in short, the present municipality is no more Swiss than South Sea Island.

Not that all these good people merely served to make the grass a little ranker here and there in odd places of the district. A number, when they could not stand it any longer, got rid of their lots as best they might, and escaped. With the persistent industry, patience, probity, and tenacity of their countrymen, not a few, or their immediate descendants, worked themselves up to a position of ease, nay, even of wealth. At the present day the

* The number is given smaller by one authority, *i.e.*, 123 in 16 months.

vicinity of Cantagallo has descendants of several of the survivors of the abandoned colony as well-to-do local Fazendeiros (planters), and there are names held good on Rio Exchange for exceptionally large sums which occurred on that obliterated list of immigrants. But it required tough constitutions and stubborn characters indeed to ensure these successes of the second generation. The colony itself was predestined to failure from its first conception. Credulous Mr. Gachet, the Swiss agent, who negotiated with Zoão VI., probably little thought, when land in the fertile *district* of Cantagallo was stipulated, that the selection would fall on spots where wastes of hungry fern and slopes of granite grit take up so large a portion of the surface. Nor could he foresee that the promised seeds and cattle would be forthcoming only in the scantiest doles, or even sometimes not at all.

When a fire gets low we put more wood on it; a dying colony wants more precious fuel to wake it up. In 1823 Messrs. Kretschmar and Schöfer procured a fresh holocaust of 342 victims for Nova Fribourgo. They had embarked in Europe trusting to contracts which ensured them fertile lands on the rivers Caravellas and Viçoso. Arrived in Rio, after 180 days of the brig 'Argos,' there was, as may be imagined, little difficulty in marching them off to the sterile heights of New Fribourg; they were meek enough by that time, and resistance under such circumstances vain at any. Though connected with a Swiss colony, this last batch of beings was composed of Germans.

Things reached such a pitch in the various Swiss colonies in Brazil, and especially the system of parceria, or Metayer, under which many citizens of the Confederation were engaged, gave rise to so many abuses, that, in 1857, the Federal Government were induced to send out a minister, in the person of the well-known and distinguished J. von Tschudi, to examine into the state of the case. Mr. von Tschudi was not the man to sit in Rio and judge from hearsay; he came to his conclusions on the sites of the colonies themselves. In the province of Espirito Santo, he found the soil and situation of the colonies for the most part bad; that the surveying engineers in some cases pocketed their salaries and contented themselves with eye measurements, and that the Directors had been usually unfit persons, sometimes rogues. In the colony of Santa Leopoldina, no one single colonist had obtained his proper share of land. All the soil is spoken of as inferior, and the Swiss minister says, that at the period of his visit, in 1860, there was not a single family so situated as to be able to support life out of the produce of their allotment. The invariable answer from the colonists, to his inquiries. of how they were getting on, was, "schlecht sehr schlecht." One man told him he had done much better with six groschen (7*d*.) in Germany than with four patacs in Brazil. These complaints were no doubt, as Tschudi admits, often exaggerated, sometimes unfounded; but however much be skimmed off on this account, there will always be a very foul remainder; hard facts which no fumes of argument can dissipate.

Another Swiss colony in Espirito Santo, visited on this occasion, was of that Rio Novo, the creation of Major Dias da Silva and Co. Its foundation had likewise been preceded by the usual rosy pamphlet; portions of *already cultivated land* had been promised, with houses ready built, &c., and there had been alluring estimates added, showing in figures the flourishing future assured to happy colonists. All falsehood and delusion, the most fortunate part of which is that they failed on this occasion to deceive many. Still twelve Swiss families are, from a Swiss point of view at least, more than a trifle after all. Tschudi characterizes the complaints of the colonists with which he was greeted in this place as an endless representation of knaveries, violence, injustice, and lies.

Though this miserable colony at least was situated on good soil in a fairly healthy locality, between the rivers Itapoana and Rio Novo, the colonists found on arrival that the virgin woods still stood up in all their glory, and that the previous cultivation spoken of in the advertisement had been a simple bait for simple folk. As Major Dias da Silva lied himself into the scrape, so he hoped to lie himself out of it. He endeavoured to excuse himself on the ground of not being prepared! But this very fact, brought forward in extenuation, was itself a formidable count of the indictment, and his appeal to it all the more barefaced, that he had six months previously professed, through his agents, that he had already made the necessary preparations for from thirty to forty families.

Mr. Tschudi found it his duty to make representations to the central Government, respecting the wretched state of the colony of Santa Leopoldina, and at the very time he was doing so, beheld its condition described in official reports as regular, and its future depicted as flattering.

Some of the most painful experiences of the Swiss are to be found among the parceria, or Metayer, settlements of São Paolo.* Most of these were visited in detail by Mr. Tschudi, who may be so far regarded as an impartial witness, that he was actually accused in the German press of having accepted bribes from the Fazendeiros to represent their case favourably. He finds that there existed faults and just causes of complaint on both sides, as no doubt there were; but as the object of this inquiry is not to bring an indictment against

* There were also parceria establishments in the Province of Rio de Janeiro in 1855.

Brazilian landowners, but rather impartially to determine the facts concerning past emigration to that country for future guidance, we may really hurry by all such defence as is based on recrimination. An admirer of the system of parceria in principle, the Swiss envoy nevertheless comes to the conclusion that the evil influences and cankerous abuses under which it is liable to suffer in Brazil are so fatal that he cannot advocate it in that country (Tschudi's Reise, vol. iii., page 259).

In Sergipe, Bahia, Alagoas, Pernambuco, &c., arrangements on the Metayer principle have long existed. Especially in the sugar districts of Brazil the proprietors of the soil allow settlers (usually Brazilians) to occupy and cultivate patches of land, bringing their cane to the Fazendeiro's mill, and receiving one-half of the sugar produced. These squatters are called Lavradores. There is another peculiar kind of labour trade carried on with indigent Portuguese and Islanders, brought out on speculation by captains of ships sailing to Brazil. These penniless individuals are ransomed from the captains by Fazendeiros on the look-out for hands, and in order to purchase their release from the ships they agree to serve any landowners who advance the amount of their debts to the skipper, till they have repaid the expenses of their journey. This they usually succeed in doing in about two years, during which time they are treated much as the blacks.

They often, however, remain on after they are free, working by agreement for wages. Being of the Latin race, they are both less exigent of comforts, and on a better footing of mutual understanding with their employers than could ever be hoped for in the case of Teutonic labourers.

The first attempt to apply this system on a large scale to Europeans, was made by the well-known Senator Vergueiro, in 1841, with ninety Portuguese families—an experiment which failed completely, in consequence of political tumults in the province. It was however renewed in 1846 with Germans, and appears, by all accounts, to have been a fair success. But after Senator Vergueiro came his son Jose, a very different sort of man, who undertook, besides meeting the demand for labour on his own fazendas, to furnish European labourers for his neighbours, to whom the total abolition of the slave trade, which occurred about 1850, had made the question of supply one of increasing embarrassment. No less than thirty-seven estates obtained labourers in this manner, so that in 1857 the total number of Europeans employed on them had reached 3600.

By the conditions of these latter contracts, according to the reasonable interpretation put on them, the colonists had to be received and brought to the place of destination by the Company Vergueiro, and receive from them all that they required, including provisions, until able to provide for themselves. Each father of a family was to have as many coffee-trees alloted to him as he could undertake the charge of, and likewise a proper piece of land for the purpose of growing articles of food. On the other hand, the colonists were bound to repay all sums supplied to or for them, whether for the journey, food, or other advances, with an interest of 6 per cent. *from the day of payment*; and to this end were bound to make over to their employer at least one-half of each year's earnings. By a provision, moreover, that gave rise to much misery, the entire family was held individually responsible for the whole amount of its debts to the planter and agents. All the colonists believed, furthermore, that the expenses of the land journey to their final destination would, by their interpretation of the contract, be borne by the Company, and were painfully surprised when the cost of their support in Santos, and during fourteen or more days' land journey, was entered as an item on their accounts. Finally, they had to pay rent for their houses, and, on Vergueiro's estate, to give up half the produce of their garden allotments to help to clear off their debt.

Hard as were many of the above conditions, had they been loyally, leave alone liberally, carried out, they would never have brought matters to the extremities at which they arrived. But, besides these burdens on the emigrants, Jose Vergueiro levied head mail in the shape of a commission of $10 per adult (1*l*.), and $5 per child, not only on those colonists he procured for other estates, but on those he obtained for himself! Nay, even for the dead that perished on the way, a commission was charged and carried with interest to the account of the survivors. This interest at 6 per cent. was charged on every advance, whether in money or kind, and sometimes on advances made by the Swiss communes for the journeys of their citizens, under the special understanding that they were to be free from interest. The colonists, moreover, often complained of the largeness of the measures used to estimate their coffee crops; of the shortness of the weights employed on the settlement stores from which they obtained their supplies; of their coffee (Fazenda Independencia) being calculated at too low a figure—their purchases too high; of their plots of land being too far from their dwellings to be useful; of an insufficient number of trees or of old trees being given over to them, with a view to delaying their emancipation; of the farce of arbitration by local Brazilian authorities in matters of dispute, and sometimes of intimidation and brutality on the part of the directors of these settlements. Perhaps, however, the most revolting part of these agreements was the fact that the colonists might be passed on from one fazenda or estate to another, with their debts, like any other transferable or negotiable article.

c 2

Often, no doubt, the complaints were exaggerated or altogether unfounded; still, enough of rigid fact, both in the conditions themselves and the mode in which they were carried out, remains to account for the outbreaks which finally occurred among the colonists, first in the State of Nova Olinda, and finally on Vergueiro's own property, Ibicaba. The latter occurred in 1856, and was a regular appeal to arms. Had it not been for the tact and prudence of those who endeavoured to restore order, not excepting Vergueiro himself, the small body of Brazilian soldiers present might have made a very awkward acquaintance with the descendants of the men of Laupen and St. Jâques. The crisis was the more perilous since the discontented denizens of other neighbouring establishments were only awaiting the issue at Ibicaba to follow suit. In both cases the rioters were all Swiss, a sense of discipline or other motives keeping the Germans in the background. The colonists of Nova Olinda were removed to Espirito Santo by the Government, and commissions of inquiry were appointed to examine the complaints; but the scandal after a short time became, notwithstanding, notorious enough to affect the trade. After 1857 no more parceria colonists came from those countries which had furnished them hitherto; altogether, far fewer were introduced, and these no longer through the hands of Vergueiro and Co.

Many of the colonists took nine years to pay their

debts. A loyal attention to the spirit of their agreement would have, and in many cases did, shorten this period considerably; so that Mr. Tschudi, at the time of his journey in 1861, found a fair proportion of hard-working emigrants already free; still, notwithstanding these happier examples, the condition of many emigrants became one of hopeless serfdom. Colonists who attempted to run away were seized, and suffered to linger in the provincial prisons, and as late as 1866 there were families whose debts, contracted in 1853, were not yet liquidated! What contributed not a little to this prolongation of bondage was the disgraceful conduct of Vergueiro. This company had bound itself to repay the communes from which the emigrants were obtained the amount of passage and other moneys advanced to their countrymen, and for this purpose received, either directly from the colonists, or indirectly through the planters to whom they had been made over, various sums of money towards the gradual extinction of their debt. Many communes, taking pity on the hard lot of their children, and perceiving what a very different matter the task of achieving independence really proved to what they had been led to anticipate, graciously remitted the debts due to them with a view to hastening the day of freedom. But Senhor Vergueiro, into whose hands these sums* had mean-

---

* This payment into the hands of Vergueiro often took place on the occasion of the transfer of the emigrants to other hands.

while passed, deliberately confiscated them to the amount of some 180,000 francs, for his own use, to indemnify himself, as he alleged, for the results of the revolt of Ibicaba, and for the loss he had sustained by the many unserviceable (halt and maimed) individuals which the communes had supplied!

Though the existence of a certain proportion of decrepid and vagabond individuals in the various batches of colonists does not testify to the good faith or good sense of the communes, which had thus sought to be rid of their bad stock, the fact cannot possibly be tortured into an excuse for robbing the innocent and robust. In general, however, it is to the bad class of colonists selected, including many disreputable, vagabond, and infirm individuals, that Mr. von Tschudi attributes the most crying evils of these Metayer enterprises of Saŏ Paolo, and bad as were the conditions, and sometimes the execution of the contracts, industrious, steady families did certainly in time work themselves free and purchase land of their own. Nor is it so much the conduct of the proprietors of the land (who, with a few exceptions, seem to have adhered pretty closely, if sometimes harshly, to the terms of their bond), but rather the altogether vicious nature of the pact itself, which is mainly answerable for the evil. The Fazendeiros naturally looked closely after their own interests, but such men as Visconde de Baependy, de Souza Barros, Texeira de Nogueira, and Senhor

Camargo were not likely to be either grasping or inhumane; while many were the acts of benevolence for which the emigrants had to thank the kindness natural to so many Brazilians.

The trial was bound to fail. Whatever may be said in favour of the Metayer system in the abstract, its adoption as the basis of the relations between the Brazilian landlord and the German emigrant seeking an Eldorado, was an experiment the results of which were not hard to foretell. The principle is only half the experiment; the matter is equally important. Plants, for instance, may no doubt be successfully grafted on one another,—not therefore the cabbage on the cactus. From its very nature the Metayer system, if it is to result in justice and satisfaction to both parties, requires a basis of mutual comprehension and confidence, a condition which, in the countries where it has been more or less successful, has been the work of traditional custom, dating from immemorial time. If, when there is identity of local origin, race, customs, and religion, the tenant is still, as we know really happens, not unfrequently left to the clemency of the landlord for the means of subsistence, what are we to expect where none of these elements show the smallest affinity, and the relation is inaugurated with grounds for mutual suspicion and disappointment? Men who seek to better their condition by emigration are not in any case likely to be contented with labouring as bond-servants for years on a soil which they can never hope to call their own. But instead of starting free, even under these circumstances, the parceria colonists commence their new existence under an incubus of debt, incurred for their passage and other expenses, from which the weakest struggle in vain to get clear. The fact that this state of serfdom for debt is voluntarily assumed does little to diminish its painful and disheartening character. It was with a sense of the inadvisability of such conditions that the North American Republic forbad, in 1864, all contract engagements of the service of emigrants *for more than a year* in payment of the costs of their importation. Philosophers may say what they like, but men do require protection from themselves, especially when hungry. If Beelzebub in full satanicals were actually to open a bureau at Hyde Park Corner for the purchase of souls, it would, after the first half-hour's shyness, be crowded from morning till night. Unfortunately, no law prevented the engagements of the half-crop colonists of Saŏ Paolo, and a member of the Sociedade Internacional de Immigração, Mr. H. Haupt, the German consul in Rio, could in 1867 report no better of them than that " the greater part of the colonists of Saŏ Paolo are irremediably enslaved by the system of parceria, notwithstanding the many sacrifices made by those European communities to which they belonged to effect their liberation from these contracts." Like the Greek agricultural population of the time of Solon, the unfortunate emigrants became something very like slaves of their creditors, having no hope short of a Seisachtheia. Thus the Government has in some instances been compelled to obtain the freedom of the colonists from their engagements, and to remove them to new centres, bringing, by these measures, some relief to their distress; but the example remains none the less prominent as a warning.

The·case of a Mr. Robillard, indeed, shows that even when both the nature of the contract and the personality of the proprietor were as favourable as possible to the emigrants, they might still, under a like or analogous system, become their own enemies, and work out nothing but ill blood and loss to both contracting parties. Mr. Robillard was no Brazilian slaveholder, and all the objectionable clauses alluded to above were wanting in his contracts. On his coffee estate at Ubatuba, he settled eight families of Fribourgeois Swiss, allowing them free lodging and garden land, and in every way liberal conditions. To the care of each family were made over as many coffee-trees as it could take charge of, for which they were expected to pay rent at the rate of $50* a year per 1000 trees. Mr. von Tschudi, from whom this case is cited, estimates that

* About 5l.

each family could, with reasonable industry, have obtained from this source alone, after payment of all rent, an income of from $400 to $600 per annum.* But so little did the colonists fulfil their part of the bargain, that during the five years in which Mr. Robillard's patience endured their presence, they never paid him one penny for the trees, and when at length he decided to get rid of them at any price —making them in fact a present of 550*l.* of debts— they cut up and injured the plantations, and indignantly complained to the Swiss envoy of the treatment *they* had received.

I mention this, because whilst showing none the less the vice apparently inherent in the system of tenant colonies in Brazil as far as yet tested, it proves that there is an altera pars, when blame is discussed, who may have a good deal to say. But a fight is none the less a fight because both parties break their heads in it, and the question of " Who's to blame ?" is not the one with which we are now most immediately concerned.

Thus much of Switzerland's experiences. There are Swiss settled in other colonies, and Swiss everywhere, and with the energy, frugality, patience, and plain sense of their race, there are very many that are doing well; but it is rather in spite of, than thanks to, their circumstances, and even thus only a portion passed out unscathed from the gauntlet of troubles and privations.

* 40*l.* to 60*l.*, or more.

I have said that Italians and French appear to have been in general exempted from furnishing the material for these numerous experiments; there are, however, some exceptions. First, I will cite the case of some former subjects of the King of Italy, now citizens of France, selected in 1855–6, for the most cruel holocaust of all.

It must always be remembered that terms that read fairly well by the dim light of the north, when they get the Tropic sun to shine on them, spell nothing but misery and semi-starvation. Mindful of this, we can understand how the following conditions proposed by a Portuguese speculator, at once found at the foot of the Alps, abundant subscribers, who, if they could have interpreted them by the light of their after experience, would have very much preferred eating them, and perhaps the proposer likewise.

These conditions, according to Consul Haupt, were:—

1. Engagements for three years.
2. Lodging and food gratis.
3. Salary of 300 francs a year.
4. Victuals to be stopped in case of illness, and medical attendance to be at the cost of the sick.
5. The right reserved to the agent to transfer their services to anyone else.

To say nothing of the extreme vagueness of the expressions "food and lodging," especially in the eyes of a speculator in human flesh, the task of supplying themselves with clothes at South American prices, and paying the doctor's bill in the climate of the Brazilian capital and its suburbs, soon taught these poor fellows that the value of money is a very relative matter indeed. But this was far from all; there remained to their consignees the right to transfer them hither and thither as might appear most profitable, and, in acting upon this right, the authors of such a scheme were not likely to be embarrassed with fond hygienic considerations in carrying it out. Nor were they. After working, by way of introduction to their new fatherland, on the Tijuca railroad, that is, along a line of country stretching from the foot of the serra of Tijuca to Rio, where the sun is usually powerful enough to addle a head of brass, they were removed to the marshes of Belem, to labour in the construction of another railroad, that of Dom Pedro II. This latter runs at first through the deadly regions of plains and swamps which intervene between serra and sea in most tropical American countries. Under the circumstances, the majority of the new workmen—stout, sinewy fellows still—did the only thing that could have been expected of them, drove their picks and mattocks bravely for a space, and then laid them away for ever. One by one, the gang of mountaineers sank into the soil they were turning; but, unfortunately, not before they had suffered an anguish of depression from the heavy air, such as only those can appreciate who have breathed both it and the free breezes of the Alps. It appears that in this way all but a thin remnant of the venture were used up, so that it can scarce have paid sufficiently to tempt the scandal of a repetition with such perishable wares. And now looking, as they often must, from some gap in the serra on the shroud of deadly mist that wraps the uncongenial resting-places of these mountaineers, and watching, here and there, those uneasy heavings of its broad surface that come with the first morning air, do no Brazilians ever think they see the wraiths of these deluded Savoyards arising to claim vengeance on the land that suffered them to be thus immolated? No Brazilian does: but the Erinnyes know better.

In 1850, a French doctor, of some reputation, of the name of Faivre, founded a colony entirely composed of his countrymen on the river Ivahy, in the province of Parana. It received considerable pecuniary assistance from the State, but was left without roads, and being situated a long way from any market and from the coast, it never prospered, and is now almost entirely dispersed. Besides this nucleus, there were a few French Alsatians in Nova Petropolis, and here and there a couple in other colonies, in Joinville, Santa Cruz, S. Angelos, Superaguy, and Santa Leopoldina. Finally, Mr. Robillard, of whom we have already spoken, was himself a Frenchman, and included some compatriots in his unsuccessful experiment above alluded to. This is, I believe, the entire extent to which France has contributed to replenishing the wilds of Brazil, and her people may on the whole congratulate themselves.

Holland is, as far as I know, only interested to the amount of a few families, in Joinville and Rio Novo, 13 in Theresopolis of Santa Catharina, 59 in Nova Petropolis of Rio Grande, 201 in Santa Maria da Solidade, and in the very questionable settlement of Santa Leopoldina, in Espirito Santo, of which mention has already been made. In the latter there were a few years ago 200 Dutchmen. They appear to have had to pay high for their land in this ill-situated colony; their houses, duly provided according to their contracts, came down for the most part on their heads, no less than thirteen directors were inflicted on them in ten years, and eight years after the establishment of the colony the Protestant inhabitants had neither chapel, school, nor clergyman.

Belgium chiefly derives her experiences from a colony on the Itajahy, in the province of Santa Catharina. It was founded in 1844, by Major von Lede, with 122 individuals. It did not get on, some colonists went back, and at one time the settlement was nearly abandoned. Poverty and necessity seem, however, to have done what State nurture in so many instances failed to effect. The Major's funds came to an end. The remaining emigrants consequently found they had to buckle to in good earnest; and thus left to its own energies, the little community seems to a certain extent to have recovered. Some Germans were added, to replace those who had returned to Europe, and a few years ago the colony appeared to be doing well. A certain number of Belgians were sent to Joinville, but they were a sorry troop, and few remained. There are fourteen Belgians in Saõ Angelo of Rio Grande, and others in Rio Novo and in Santa Cruz of the same province. The only other Belgian enterprise of this kind which I am aware of is the project of Señhora von Langendorf to establish a colony on the Serra Negra, in Assunguy, Parana. I know nothing of its results. Like the French and Italians the Belgians may be found sporadically among settlements of other nations.

The motley colony of Santa Leopoldina formerly contained seventy Tyrolians, who are better off than their neighbours, except in so far as they are Catholics.

Of the Portuguese, besides the regular influx, so much of which as we have seen flows back—and besides the numbers brought out by speculation of various kinds and distributed among the fazendas—there have been regular colonies at different intervals. But, though one might have expected to find at least the countrymen of Cabral at home and flourishing, the Portuguese nuclei give so little encouragement that it can scarce be doubted that the inhabitants of the mother-country are much better left to find their own way out to Brazil and their own place when there. As navvies, stonecutters, artizans, they find no difficulty in establishing themselves, and set a praiseworthy example of honest work; as colonists they do not appear to satisfy either themselves or their sponsors much better than other nations. Thus we have Santa Isabel of Maranhaõ, founded in 1853, Nossa Señhora de O' in Para, dating from 1854, Sinimbú and Engenho Novo, of 1859, in Bahia, all of Portuguese, or with some admixture of natives, and all, more or less, complete failures, the Portuguese slinking away. Again, in 1855, a parceria attempt with Portuguese was made in Maranhão. Nine hundred and eleven were distributed over six stations, a number which, in 1857, had sunk to 359, and has since dwindled still more. The late Baron de Nova Fribourgo also obtained but poor results with the Portuguese; an eloquent testimony—seeing that here race, language, customs, and religion were alike—of the indubitable something rotten in the application of this system in Brazil.

As to Spaniards, they are likely to resort to the country when caterpillars colonize ants' nests, and owls foxes' earths. Besides, they have yet a fair island or so of their own, when they feel restless, without troubling either their secular enemies or their own unnatural children.

We have now come to the country that has by far the greatest interest in the question of Brazilian emigration, and whose participation in it has at length reached proportions to which historical importance can no longer be denied. This country is Germany, with whose sons the earliest regular attempt at colonization, after that of Nova Fribourgo, was made in 1825, at Saõ Leopoldo, in the province of Rio Grande. In 1850 the total number of persons, of all nationalities, in all the colonies of the empire was estimated at 18,760 souls (Tavares Bastos). In 1860 the German population of the municipality of Saõ Leopoldo alone counted 12,500 inhabitants; while Mr. von Tschudi, at the time of his visit, estimated the additional numbers, which had spread from this place over the province (of Saõ Pedro de Rio Grande do Sul) at between 16,000 and 18,000. At the present day the Teutonic element is 42,789 strong in that province; and the total number of Germans in Brazil about 77,000 souls. This northern stock has been implanted in the following distinct nuclei, most of which are almost entirely German:—

Saõ Leopoldo, in Rio Grande .. .. founded 1824-5
Tres Forquilhas, in Rio Grande .. .. ,, 1826
Saõ Pedro de Alcantara das Torres, in Rio Grande ,, 1826
Saõ Pedro de Alcantara, in Santa Catharina .. .. ,, 1827-8
Rio Negro, founded with disbanded German soldiers but dwindled away almost to nothing, in Province of Parana .. .. ,, 1828

Petropolis, Rio de Janeiro	founded	1846
Santa Isabel, in Santa Catharina	,,	1845
Santa Isabel, in Espirito Santo	,,	1847
Nossa Senhora da Piedade (wound up as a failure), in Santa Catharina	,,	1847
Santa Cruz, in Rio Grande	,,	1849
Rincão del Re of Germans from S. Leopoldo, in Rio Grande	,,	1850
Mundo Novo, in Rio Grande	,,	1850
Blumenau, in Santa Catharina	,,	1850
Dona Francesca, in Santa Catharina	,,	1851
Mucury, in Minas Geraes	,,	1852
In many of the thirty-seven parceria colonies, in Saõ Paolo	,,	1852
Conventos, in Rio Grande	,,	1854
In Independencia and other fazendas on the parceria system, in Rio de Janeiro	,,	1855
Santa Leopoldina, in the Province of Espirito Santo	,,	1856
Rio Novo, probably only a few Germans, in the Province of Espirito Santo	,,	1856
Estrella, four Bavarians, in the Province of Rio Grande	,,	1856
Transylvania, in the Province of Espirito Santo	,,	1856
Saõ Angelo, in the Province of Rio Grande	,,	1857
Santa Maria da boca do Monte, founded by S. Leopoldo colonists, in the Province of Rio Grande	,,	1857
Santa Maria da Soledade, or Montravel, in the Province of Rio Grande	,,	1857
Nova Petropolis, including, I believe, Santa Theresa on the Cahy, in the Province of Rio Grande	,,	1858
Saõ Lourenço, in the Province of Rio Grande	,,	1858
Theresopolis of Santa Catharina, in the Province of Rio Grande	,,	1860
Dom Pedro II., or Juiz da Fora, in Minas, in the Province of Rio Grande	,,	1860
Itajahy, in the Province of Santa Catharina	,,	1860
Taquary, or Teutonia, private colony founded by German merchants, in the Province of Rio Grande Assunguy, Parana	,,	1860

In all 30 colonial centres, besides the numerous Metayer settlements in Saõ Paolo and Rio de Janeiro.

Cahy, of which I also find mention among my papers, is probably Santa Theresa, on the Cahy

Covitiba. A few of the above colonies, as Estrella for instance, have very few German inhabitants; and there are, no doubt, odd Germans in others not mentioned, besides which there are some 2000 in the town of Rio de Janeiro, and others scattered through the country.

Whether, now, we look at its extent, its early date and persistent recurrence; to numbers, to the energy of race, or to the results obtained, the German colonization of Brazil is by far the most important attempt yet made to populate that country by Europeans other than the owners, and constitutes a phenomena of no small historical significance.

As to the results, they are the fairest, and the future of these settlements is the most hopeful in all that dark calendar of error, recklessness, and speculation.

Above all, it would seem that German colonization, at whatever cost, has finally taken root as a living fact, likely to bear fruit in due season, and is no longer washed backwards and forwards on the uncertain current of experiment. Twenty or thirty years ago, the life of a German labouring man was not what it now is, or is fast becoming. Small states had stern laws, and, in the larger ones, multitudinous restrictions gave little room for free expansion. Trade, throttled in its mediæval swathing-clothes, was often dull, prices and wages low, manufactures, in some states, in something like to infancy; thereto came political dissensions, military service, bad harvests, with hunger-typhus in the rear; so that a poor man might well come, and that not seldom, to feel pinched. Thus the devil drove; the desire of those who ruled the councils of Brazil to replenish their land opened a way. After the formal denunciation, followed, about 1850, by the practical suppression of the slave trade, this dilettante desire became an imperative necessity; henceforward agents were constantly at hand in Europe, with all their paraphernalia of puffs, placards, and pamphlets, to assist the harassed German in his attempt to escape a bitter present, to allure him with sunny pictures of the future.

In sooth it was a real case of needs must, and the two necessities played perfectly into each other. Ship after ship disembarked its human cargo, colony followed colony into the bowers of the Eldorado. Now the lot fell on slopes of scarped granite; now in the recesses of some fertile nook; now on some breezy albeit barren heights; now in the chokedamp of some matted wood; now the auspices were taken by a nobler enthusiast; now all depended on some lord of nigger hordes. Petropolis and Santa Leopoldina, Juiz da Fora and Mucury, Blumenau and Angelica, all had their turn, and some their victims, but still the German emigration flowed on. As a bare rock surface over which the water trickles, nothing seems to hold, nothing to flourish on it. But let at length but one chance seed catch in an inequality, lodge on a vantage-ground, and the inhospitality even of that blank surface is vanquished, an oasis is formed. Plenty of reinforcements and the impossibility of retreat will carry any position. Contracts proved false, authorities partial, soils barren, climates lethal, measurements faulty, payments slack, sympathies scanty, laws and religion alien, while the labourer savoured no sweeter than elsewhere; but German discontent still drove, German industry and German frugality survived this and more; until at last, for weal or woe, this race seems to have really won a footing in the country.

One great element in the comparatively satisfactory results which have attended German colonization is the fortunate locality in which half of the settlements have been established, namely, the temperate and congenial province of Rio Grande. Santa Catharina and Parana also boast well-to-do colonies; and but a few experiments have been made in the altogether unsuitable lowlands of the tropics.

But it is our duty, while gladly marking the flecks of green which at last brighten the rock, to note the waste of seed that drifted nowhere; the starved growth that sprung up only to wither. German experience would form a catalogue of all the ills of Brazilian colonization, ills which are summed up elsewhere. It was the enlightened desire of Dom Pedro I. to establish German colonies in Brazil, that led to the earliest importation of that nationality, consisting of 126 individuals. These arrived in 1824, and were shortly followed by others, so that by 1830 the total number had reached 4856 souls. These colonists were established in a favourable locality on the Rio dos Sinas in Rio Grande, on a spot where a royal establishment for the culture of hemp and flax had formerly been situated. The lands were given gratuitously, and in addition the settlers received an allowance of 320 reis a day per person for the first, 160 reis for the second year, besides seeds, implements, and cattle. Thus originated the now celebrated, and, after many vicissitudes, undoubtedly successful colony of Saõ Leopoldo, at present a district with a municipal town alone numbering 3000 souls, and a centre of the highest importance to the future of colonization and of the province. From the very first there were complaints of the measurements of the allotments, and forty years later there were colonists without proper titles to their lands; at times, too, the direction of the colony, especially in the days of one Lima, appears to have been of the wantonest. There were complaints of overreaching, tyranny, and dissolute conduct of the authorities. At the same time, the early colonists appear themselves to have been no angels, and some were undoubtedly jail birds, whose fetters were slipped at the moment of exportation.

Brilliant results were, under the circumstances, hardly to be expected, even had no civil war broken out in 1835. Still the hardy nucleus persisted. From 1831 to 1844 no new colonies came to the province of Rio Grande. The nine years of revolutionary conflict, from which the Germans at first kept aloof, eventually split them into two parties, one for the Government, one for the insurgents, and from this time they seem to have persecuted and destroyed each other with as sound internecine feelings as any of the natives. In 1844 the Germans commenced coming again, and the nucleus began in time to use an attractive force from its own bulk and reputation worth all the artificial influence of mendacious agencies. There were still troubles enough to be borne, hard work to be done, and hardships to be endured, but the painted figments of an Eldorado of idleness had been cleared away, and colonization looked at in its real light. Things worked steadily on from bad to better. Among other troubles the attacks and depredations of the Indians, though not so serious as in La Plata districts, cannot be altogether passed over, especially since they are rather to be estimated by the anxious vigilance they demand than from the actual evil they can succeed in inflicting upon a brave and alert people. Still from time to time victims fell under the arrows of the hostile aborigines; in one attack, indeed, no less than eleven persons; and as late as 1864, I read of one Johann Klink, of the neighbouring settlement of Nova Petropolis, who was interrupted in his victuals by the sudden ping of an arrow that pinned his garments to his flesh.

The colony, however, worked through; the seed clung to the rock face, drove sturdy fibres into its chinks, and Brazil is justified in claiming what credit she may from its present exceptionally favourable aspect. Though producing little or nothing of the staple riches of the tropics, São Leopoldo more than retrieves this shortcoming in advantages of climate; while maize, mandioca, tobacco, rice, flax, hemp, sugar, peas, beans, wheat, and vines, give no niggard variety of culture. In 1843 the value of the agricultural produce sent out from the colony was about $300,000*; a sum which in 1861 had reached $3,000,000†; and the municipal revenue at this latter time was no less than $24,000 to $27,000, or about 2700*l*. "Enemies of Brazilian colonization," says Mr. Tschudi, "should at any rate just ask in this colony how many of the colonists would exchange their present lot with their former one in Germany, or how many have any desire at all to return to their old home."

---

* Over 30,000*l*.   † Over 300,000*l*.

This first glimpse is of the good side, to count the costs minutely would be a long affair; they were much such as were paid by other nations. Here are, however, a few specimens both of the more remarkable among successful settlements and of the more lamentable frauds and failures.

In 1845 was created that miserable delusion, that imperial starveling, the colony of Petropolis; situated in a locality bearing the ominous name of " Corrego seco," " the dry stream." Here on narrow slopes of crumbling gneiss, always between a torrent and a crag, was founded one of the most numerous German settlements of the empire, and here German assiduity and sobriety have managed, and still manage, to subsist on meagre thankless plots of ground. But even this poor result is only owing to the artificial stimulus of the Emperor's summer residence, to the money brought by wealthy excursionists flying the heats of Rio. The same influences also suffice to keep up trade on the Aegishorn, and the want of them settles the fate of such localities as Nova Fribourgo and Theresopolis.

Poor as was the choice, unsound as proved the direction of many Government colonies, the greatest prejudice, both to the reputation of Brazil and to the fate of individuals, resulted from private speculators and unscrupulous agents. In 1846 came the first utterance of the accumulated sense of wrong, in a correspondence between Herr Kanitz and the

Visconde de Abrantes, Brazilian minister at Berlin. In one of the notes exchanged on this occasion, the latter (as quoted by Consul Haupt) expresses himself strongly against what he styles the "system of seduction," and against companies, agencies, and speculators generally, admitting by implication the validity of the complaints then urged against them. While endeavouring to exculpate his Government, he stigmatizes emphatically and effectually one of the commonest forms of Brazilian colonization projects—one of which Englishmen have lately had sad enough experience.

Not that all enterprise of this kind, conducted by private individuals, was equally nefarious. Very far from it: as we have some of the worst so we have some of the happiest projects among those originally due to private initiative. Among the better kind of work done in this way, we may mention that of the União colonizadoria de Hamburgo, a society formed, in 1849, with a view to turn part of the flowing tide of emigration of that period towards Brazil. Not every society could rely on such princely resources or such high protection. The Prince de Joinville possessed by right of his wife, a Brazilian princess, a large but waste territory in the province of Santa Catharina. Of this fruitful wilderness he agreed to cede the company in question twelve square leagues for purposes of colonization, wisely assuming that he would, by this cession, vastly increase the value of the portion retained by him. The moment selected for the enterprise was propitious, and the labours of the association were soon apparent in the foundation (in 1851) of Dona Francesca, or Joinville.*

This colony seems from the first to have caught something of the air of its high sponsors. It certainly consumed great sums of money, drawing largely both on the Society and the Princes of the House of Orleans, and the Brazilian Government, to say nothing of considerable sums obtained from the colonists themselves in purchase of their lands. In return for all this, Joinville, if it did not show very solid agricultural or financial results, offered itself for contemplation as a model, an intellectual paragon, an æsthetic nucleus, a fancy Zukunfts colony. But the attention paid by the first director to the amenities and graces of life, is thought to have been to the prejudice of ruder, more material interests, and there has been much disappointment amongst sober men as to the results obtained from this most lavishly assisted nucleus. While lands were sold at fancy prices, the colonists found it hard to live on great expectations and brilliant representations, and so, at one time, a great number left the colony. Still, the climate, notwithstanding some endemic fever at one time, is fair, with cool

* The Duc D'Aumale, as well as the Prince de Joinville, was concerned in the matter, I believe.

nights and occasional frosts, the soil is in parts good, and there are now good roads. Altogether, therefore, though somewhat cramped in its development by the avowed intention of the Grand Seigneur not to sell his lands, but only to grant perpetual leases, Dona Francesca, or Joinville, is no failure, and, with an actual population of between 4000 or 5000 souls, looks forward to a future of solid prosperity.

One of the most flourishing of German colonies, Blumenau, in Santa Catharina, is in its origin even more thoroughly a private enterprise, and was entirely the offspring of individual energy. But a man of such integrity and generous enthusiasm as Herr Blumenau, the Brunswicker, is an unique apparition in the chronicles of Brazilian colonization. The necessary lands were obtained partly by purchase, partly by state gift, in a healthy fertile neighbourhood on the river Itajahy, which serves as an admirable means of communication. A nucleus of Germans had already been established in the neighbourhood as early as 1827. It is known as the "old German colony," and was formed of a portion of the colonists brought out by Major Scheffer, the man who had been so active in procuring colonists for São Leopoldo. Herr Blumenau proceeded very cautiously in settling colonists in his domain, beginning with only seventeen persons. Altogether he introduced as many as 834, and in

1864 the census of the place gave 2471 inhabitants. But it rarely if ever happens that a Brazilian colony enjoys that exuberance of luck which might make it a success for all the three factors usually concerned in its fate, the country, the colonists, and the founder. One or more has to pay the piper. To the country and colonists Blumenau was decidedly a success; but this result was only obtained by the enthusiasm and sacrifices of the founder, who finally found himself out of pocket by no less a sum than 16,000 Prussian thalers (2400*l*.).

The country, however, which cannot but gain in the end by these enterprises, black as things may look in the interval, very properly relieved Herr Blumenau from his personal losses, indemnifying him in full. At the same time the Brazilian Government took over the colony, though it wisely retained as director the high-minded man who had originated and so far fostered it.

The first volunteers obtained in the province for the Paraguayan war marched from Blumenau.

In the same district, on the little Itajahy, a stream far less to be relied on for navigation, there was formed, in 1861, the Government colony of Brusque. It seems to have been badly administered. In 1861 it had 406; in 1864, 938; in 1866, 1212 inhabitants. Likewise in the province of Santa Catharina, is the colony of Theresopolis, founded in 1860, having, in 1865, 1500 inhabitants, and 1530 a short time ago. Also Santa Isabel, founded in 1847, on good hilly land, with about 150 Germans; counting 284 inhabitants in 1861, and subsequently 851; and Saõ Pedro, of Alcantara, founded as long ago as 1829 on the River Mucuhy. Beginning with 523 persons, mostly Germans, to which number 93 more were shortly after added, this latter colony had, in 1844, 2000 inhabitants. It had a good deal to endure both from the animosity of Indians and jealousy of whites inhabiting the neighbourhood, the latter keeping a hold on the land, though they did not work it, and was finally emancipated and invested with municipal dignity. It is doing well, but is no Paradise of idleness.

In 1851 Senator Theophilo Benedicto Ottoni, a name sacred in Brazil, originated, with his brother Honorio, the company of navigation of the Mucuhy, with the object of benefiting their native province Minas, by a new way of communication, and a colony. The name of the projectors augured little of the evils afterwards engendered, but the point of view was essentially Brazilian, and the site of the new settlement was selected some two or three hundred miles from the coast. The surveys were so imperfect, that, only after the works had gone on three years, was the startling discovery made, that the way by the natural high road, namely the river, which it was intended to replace, extended over only 25 leagues of navigation, instead of 40, as had been estimated; whereas the new route, instead of extending for only 16 leagues, would stretch over 40!!

The effect of this discovery on the Company may be imagined. I pass on to the European point of view and the colonists. These did not arrive as freely as was expected; the Germans were getting a little shy; an agent was accordingly dispatched to Europe, and through his mediation some good colonists, with not a little trash, were procured. Relegated to the wilds, they soon experienced disgust and disappointment, resulting, in 1856, in lamentable scenes of violence. Meanwhile there had been founded in Rio de Janeiro the famous (latinice famosus) central association of colonization, the chief agency of which in Europe was the house of Beaumont, in Antwerp. These pages are not the place for sifting dirt, nor is it really of much interest to know whether the respectable house at Antwerp, or the illustrious Brazilian association, are most responsible for the monstrous impositions which were practised between them. All that now avails is so to mark the coin that it may have no chance of passing a second time without detection. To give an example, then. In a proclamation issued on the part of the association in question, we find Brazil spoken of as "that extravagantly fertile land." Now, over an immense extent, especially of those southern provinces chosen for the sites of colonies, it is gneiss tossed into hills, furrowed by gorges, scooped into narrow valleys by torrents. The decomposition of this rock, together with the mysterious agencies of the South American drift period, have in parts produced a rich aluminous paste; the rest is a lean granitic wilderness. For this latter sun and water have indeed done wonders, and have here and there piled up a fair thickness of humus, but they took æons to do it, and when it is gone, even those magicians cannot quickly vivify afresh the wastes of quartz. A little farther on the same documents assert, that "carpenters, stone-masons and joiners can earn at the least thirteen francs a day, and cultivate their lands besides." Opening the reports on the industrial classes presented to Parliament in 1870, at page 520, anyone will be enabled to judge for himself of the naïve mendacity of these agencies, especially if he consider which way wages have tended since 1857. On this page, the current wages in Brazil are given thus:—

Blacksmiths	2s. to 3s. per diem.
Carpenters	3s. ,, 4s ,,

The next sentence is better suited to burlesque than to the scenes of tragedy to which it played the prelude.

"To give an idea of the advantages awaiting emigrants to that country, a detailed account of which would be very long, it suffices to mention this one fact: shooting and fishing, which everywhere else are either strictly prohibited or exceedingly expensive, are there free, and *of great advantage to the colonists!*"

Imperial generosity! All this anybody may have gratuitously; that is, if he can catch it.

Everyone who has had experience of tropical American virgin woods knows, that for practical purposes, the game consists rather in beetles than beasts of the chase, in ferns than feathers, and in thorns and ticks than either. Now, Brazil is so far from being an exception, as far as my small experience goes, that though I took out guns, ammunition, and a retriever, I soon turned plant hunter, and never shot anything larger than a swallow the whole time I was in the country. I once saw an armadillo, occasionally the tracks of paca and tapir, now and then heard the far-off discord of parrots and monkeys above the vast dome of foliage, or caught a rare glimpse of Penelope or Inhambu, but this was all; and yet I spent a great part of my time in the forest. I took to orchids and my dog to wasps. *Some* of the streams no doubt contain abundant fish, but they do not answer to the whistle, and few persons, except Brazilians, find time to spend on enticing them. The gentle art is wisely left to Indians and creole whites, who can live on next to nothing and would live on less to save themselves from labour. Still there is more truth in the asseveration of the placard than was meant, for the shooting and fishing of Brazil might perhaps, by one who knew their value, be taken as types of the advantages assured to colonists emigrating to that empire. Meanwhile the fishers of men had baited well; a large number of unfortunates were decoyed by this agency, and dispatched to the jungle of the interior to form the colony of Philadelphia. After deceptions, disappointment, and misery had led to complaints and disturbances of all kinds, the Government interfered, and sent an agent to inquire into a state of things which had already cost many lives. The somewhat unqualified report of this functionary no doubt exists in the ministerial archives to this day; but would be difficult to obtain. It is said to have been exaggerated. At any rate the Government found itself compelled to take over the colony in 1861, and under this high protection it still vegetates. It was in the early years of the Mercury Company, 1852 *et seq.*, that the Germans made their experience of the Metayer (Parceria) establishments and of the Agency Vergueiro. They differed little from those of the Swiss already discussed, and require no further comment. They must have considerably damaged the market. The same remarks apply to the miserable imposture of Major Dias, on the Rio Novo, and to Santa Leopoldina, both founded in the province of Espirito Santo in 1856. Transylvania, of the same year and province, was a failure; after which we come to some new colonies in the provinces south of Rio, which are pulling through.

In 1863 we find the German envoy in Brazil journeying to Saõ Leopoldo to endeavour to obtain a settlement of the long-standing complaints of the colonists with respect to the measurement of their land—late justice, which he seems, by the co-operation of the Central Government, to have succeeded in procuring; and finally, in recent days, we hear of the Federal Government of Germany warning its people, through the columns of the 'Staats-Anzeiger,' against contract colonization schemes lately set on foot by the Provincial Governments of Saõ Paolo and Rio Grande do Sul.

To sum up the chequered results of German colonization, of which it has only been possible to give the narrowest of glimpses, in so far as they concern Brazilians, Germans, and the moral for Englishmen:—

Firstly, as regards Brazil, Germanism, for good or ill, has in that land become a fact; the egg, be it cockatrice or chicken, is hatched, and the best course must therefore be to cherish and attach the young, of no matter what feather. Smother it, and it will sting the best protected hand; conciliate it, and it will one day lay golden eggs.

The reason of the above remark will scarcely seem apparent to those who ignore to what extent Brazilians, until very recently, were opposed to all foreign colonization, and that the old colonial virus still elaborates a jealousy which even the stern necessities of the day fail entirely to negative. The practical power and vitality of this feeling may be gathered from the fact that in 1864 the municipality of the great German centre of Saõ Leopoldo consisted almost entirely of Brazilians, while in that of Nova Fribourga there were, in 1861, out of fifty-seven municipal functionaries, but two naturalized foreigners, although the latter class formed the majority of the population; but these times are passing away, the young is nearly fledged, and, as Mr. Tschudi remarks of Rio Grande do Sul, "Germanism has become a power against the uninterrupted growth of which the jealousy of Brazilians fights in vain."

In a financial point of view, owing to improvidence, carelessness, dilettantism, bad management, and the dishonesty of subordinates, the German colonies have cost the treasury large sums; but there can be little doubt that, though the above causes may retard the day, the industry of Teuton men and the fecundity of the women will eventually more than balance the account. Failures in all other senses, such colonies as Mucury, Petropolis, and Nova Fribourgo have been no failures for Brazil — in the fresh blood and sinew, thrift and energy dispersed over the country from these wretched centres, she at least can well afford to forget the hunger and heartsickness of the victims, the dead that in their poor way likewise enrich her soil. In the new element thus acquired, and its power of attracting reinforcements, Brazil need do nothing but congratulate herself; it is the finest in the country and the same which boasted 1800 years ago,

"Nullos mortalium armis aut fide ante Germanos esse."

Next, as to the Germans: what the Brazilians paid for in money and loss of reputation, Germany subscribed in flesh and blood, making a heavy bill against the horde of paid puffers, agents, recrutatores, speculators, and rascally directors. We have seen to what scenes and recriminations the items of this bill gave rise as they occurred. The bitter tone of the German consul's writings on the subject, though, may be, excessive, speaks for the impression produced on an intelligent man and an advocate of European colonization, in a position giving him unusual facilities for judging of the question. In Germany there has been clamour enough at various times on this head; but among it the sound of serious voices, worthy of attention, arguing honestly against emigration to Brazil; while the Government itself has, on more than one occasion, spoken distinctly and authoritatively in this sense, and especially against the schemes of private persons. Still those Germans who have held out have secured themselves an independence and a livelihood, a freedom from police, paternal restrictions, and elaborate taxation not easily attainable in their own land, though their hands keep, after all, as horny, their gait as heavy, and sometimes their stomachs as hungry as in the home of their fathers.

Pastors, professors, engineers, merchants, and representatives of most other branches of human activity have been supplied, as well as agricultural colonists—there being no less than 500 Germans in the town of Porto Allegre alone, and 2000 in the city of Rio de Janeiro,—so that Germany's stake in the country is a manifold as well as a large one. "Wer nicht nachgiebt der gewinnt." The fight has been fought and won by sheer persistence. This is an age which soon buries its dead. Whatever it cost, Germany may, on the whole, be proud of her inheritance in the well-to-do and peaceful empire of Brazil; while hard-working Germans, who have their eyes open, their pockets not quite empty, a n their minds clear of illusions, might easily go to a worse place.

And, *thirdly*, as to the moral for Englishmen. Does anyone suppose that if Germany owned one-tenth of the flourishing colonial territory of Great Britain, any appreciable number of her sons would drift to heterogeneous and alien shores? Remote aggrandizement and nautical enterprise have not been in her way of late, though her day may come. The lurking, scarce-formulated wish to Germanize on a more material basis than the hospitality of other nations may some day be realized. Meanwhile the peaceful conquest, with its growing centres, will serve as an ever more and more congenial outlet for her crowded population, as breathing-room for a great nationality beyond the narrow European pale, as a mine for her merchants, and perhaps, in time, as a ripe field for her missionaries. But an Englishman may find all this and more on much better terms, without ever going beyond the ruddy reflection of his own standard, without being called on to exchange his Penates for some uncouth gods, without submitting to the gyves and pinionings of a repugnant legislation, or to the constant fretting of abhorrent modes of life and thought. Half the estimate of a purchase is the price, and no man chooses willingly the dearest mart. We have seen the price paid by Germany for her footing in Brazil; but though necessity may warrant it in her case, this does not justify or explain the demand of Englishmen to be included in a similar bargain.

Of all the many vagaries of Brazilian colonization, the immigration from the United States was perhaps the most abnormal and peculiar. It was one baker borrowing flour of another, the brewer selling malt. Such transactions point at once to some transitory disturbance of the usual conditions of existence; and in this case the great civil war and the abolition of slavery were the elements of Brazil's opportunity. She scarcely appears to have profited by it as she ought to have done. Instead of New Orleans, it was New York that, strange to say, was made the port of exit from which free or assisted passages were granted; and an American Company, that of the "United States and Brazil Mail Ships," obtained a contract by which, for certain considerations, they engaged to import emigrants at a moderate charge. If, as is most probable, the choice of a northern port as point of departure deterred many Southerners from availing themselves of the Brazilian offers, something alluring in the proffered terms contributed not a little to make up the deficiency from other sources. In this way a considerable number of Americans reached Brazil, and were distributed among the southern provinces. Among the new comers were men with fair sums of money, exiles from the old slave States. Hatred of the North determined their departure, slavery proclivities their selection of a new home. In December, 1866, the Company's steamers landed 200 citizens of the North American Republic, and later on, some thousands more at different intervals. But this stream of immigration has, I believe, at this time, ceased altogether its unnatural course, in spite of the hyperbolical propositions occasionally brought forward by the restless speculation of the Yankee, ready to supply anything to anybody. Those that came with it, and many of whom returned soon after, gained abundant experience of the want of system, preparation, and foresight which presides over emigration matters in Brazil. There were the same heartburnings and complaints, the same distressing scenes; and, in particular, the unfortunate creatures who were exposed without proper shelter to the torrential rains and climatic influences of the month of January in Cananea, are not likely to attract others by their reports. This latter place, to which numbers both of Americans and English were at different times dispatched, was always changing its population, fresh reinforcements arriving ever and anon to fill the gaps left by those who abandoned it. In these times Rio was full of helpless Saxons, not always of the meekest temperament. The Government was assailed with reproaches, food and lodgings had to be provided, and the hospitable house of the editor of the 'Anglo-Brazilian Times,' the indefatigable champion of Brazilian emigration, harboured at most times tattered examples of the perpetual abortion of the cause for which he at all seasons so recklessly enters the lists. As with the Americans, so it was at the same period with the English, the Anglo-Saxon race seemed to show a particular impatience of what they looked upon as injustice, a desperate restlessness under the depressing influences of their new-found Paradise. Private purses were taxed for the nourishment of these luckless families during their stay in Rio de Janeiro, and sometimes for payment of their passages back to their homes, while I remember to have seen an excited crowd of my countrymen threaten Her Majesty's bachelor *chargé d'affaires*, that they would come and lay their babies on his doorsteps, if he failed to procure the satisfaction of their demands. Poor bachelor! poor babies!

At the same time North American emigration was very far from universally popular in the Empire. There was a not unnatural prejudice against the keen, hard adventurers of the North, much such as an oyster might have against admitting a nail as bedfellow—as though there were some danger of the heterogeneous element remaining segregated as gout-stones in the system: and indeed that nation of filibusters, those grey-eyed fanatics of a destiny of Empire, might well give rise to qualms and apprehensions, did they come to squat in numbers in a soft and peaceful land. Meanwhile experiences have been made on both sides, and though North American enterprise and energy is likely both to gain and bestow much profit in Brazil, it will be as the results of isolated, individual initiative, when shoal emigration from the Republic is, as I believe to be even now the case, at an end.

As after the civil war in the United States, so, too, after the last struggles of the Poles,—projects were concocted at Rio in 1865-6 for landing something from the troubled waters; but remained, as far as I know, without any appreciable results.

Danes to the number of nine appear on the list of colonists of Estrella, in the province of Rio Grande; and, strangest item of all this motley category, Dona Francesca contains a small number of Icelanders, who, notwithstanding the change of climate, are said to be doing remarkably well, and giving great satisfaction by their industry. Certainly, if in the case of British subjects also, Brazil limited her importations to any there may be roaming in the more immediate neighbourhood of the Pole, no monitory voice need have been raised.

Lean Mongolian figures lounging between two round, suspended fish-baskets, like perambulating pairs of scales, show that the universal *pis aller*, the coolie, has not been forgotten. These men are the survivors of the brutality and bad treatment heaped upon an importation of that unfortunate race which was made in 1856. An English house contracted for the introduction of 2000, but after 566 had been landed, the contract was for some reason rescinded. Nay, in her perplexity, and in view of the comparative barrenness of her union with so many foreign stocks, Brazil has even had recourse to self-fertilization, and indulged fond faith in Parthenogenesis. She has, in fact, colonized herself in several spots, Estrella, Sinimbú, Iguape, Itajahy, for instance;

and yet not even this homologous impiug has given brilliant results.

This cursory, but not one-sided, glance at the Protean forms of Brazilian colonization is now at an end, leaving, I trust, the reader capable of answering himself this question:—

Whether there be anything in the experience of other nations, or the fate of former colonies, which could justify the Englishman's adoption of so incongenial a stepmother?

But even the experience of others does not warrant the rejection of that which in itself is manifestly good. Englishmen assert the right of trying things on their own merits, for themselves, asking only in the more expensive trials, that there be some solid and certain advantage indubitably present in the background of worth sufficient to justify risk and reward success. The worth must be, moreover, higher or the risk smaller than in other ventures lying more conveniently to hand. Let us see if it be not possible to detect some such high intrinsic qualities in Brazil. And, first, let it be premised that broad characteristics and not exceptions must form the basis of our estimate, which must, furthermore, be limited to those districts practically accessible to colonists, and available for the establishment of new communities.

First, then, as to the climate.—As I was a native of the tropics, and have subsequently visited various parts, such as Central America, Darien, Peru, Marquezas, Sandwich Islands, Brazil, &c., there is some faint *primâ facie* grounds for assuming that my humble judgment of those enchanting lands will neither be tainted with prejudice nor altogether worthless from ignorance. With this premise, I would respectfully submit that, whatever wholesome influences the regions of Cancer and Capricorn may be fitted to exert on the cold, acarbonic races of the future, the fact of a place being situated within the limits of the torrid zone is *at present, cæteris paribus*, a presumption against its perfect suitability as a habitation for northern men, or for the evolution of the highest energies and noblest qualities of the human race. Only admitting altitude to produce in great measure the results of latitude, it will not require very erudite researches on the surface of the globe, or among the pages of history, to see that all experience here points one way. Indeed, any profane tourist may substantiate for himself this awful blasphemy against the sun, by Baconian "travelling instances," he need not travel far to find. In the second place, the tropics of Brazil in particular suffer from conditions which, if they be found also in some other countries, are nevertheless far from inseparable from torrid regions in general. The trade winds sweep straight from the ocean over the eastern portions of that country. No drop of water has been taken from them, and, in this saturated state, they rise to the higher levels of the maritime mountain range, where they seem to be rung by unseen hands, so sudden and tremendous is the deluge which ensues. This water tears down the valleys in destructive torrents, drenches the marches, and rises again and again in mephitic vapour, decocted of rank vegetation, and trying to human health. But far more than this is it the large amount of moisture which, at certain seasons of the year, remains suspended in the air and does *not* come down, that is so trying to European constitutions. The atmosphere and all' it envelopes seems viscid with wet, there is a clammy weight in the lightest clothes, the muscular tissue relaxes, the sense grows dull and heavy, the energies are paralyzed, healthy evaporation is checked, while *exhaled* moisture trickles from the back of the hand, the memory fails, a fretful languor makes even the involuntary continuance of purely vegetable existence irksome and distressing. In such times provisions perish, leather and other materials become spotted and mildewed, metal in use oxidizes, glue softens, plaster falls, wood warps, and man with difficulty persuades himself that he too is not yielding to the general impulse to decay, breaking up in a crop of toadstools. These influences do not fortunately continue during the whole year: in some rare districts they are perhaps altogether wanting, and in others no doubt, during many months unknown.

CLIMATE. 63

On the other hand, there are localities where this is the prevailing state of things, while even in the Serras the dry and bracing season is limited to a few months.

Another consideration with respect to the climate of Brazil is the situation of its great towns. While the Spaniards wisely placed their capitals and chief cities on the hill land, high above malaria, and far away from the swamps and noxious influences of tropic coast lines, the Portuguese founded such noble towns as Bahia, Rio, and Pernambuco on the very beach, within the everlasting haze of the foam. Between the strand on which these cities are erected and the foot of the Serra do Mar stretches a band of hot country, varying in breadth from 20 to 100 miles, containing some of the most fertile portions of soil. But unfortunately, like the fabled Hesperides, they have their dragon; for it is precisely at the foot of these tropical ranges, amidst the marshes from which they rise, that some of the most terrible fevers are met with. If the yellow Jack, with its predilections for mariners, seems to hang along the shore, the hideous effects of true malaria are mostly met with at some distance from the coast, near the spurs of the mountains. Conscious of the importance of the vicinity of some great town to agricultural colonists, and aware of the rich resources of these lower lands, it has been proposed to settle colonists in some of the more salubrious portions of this torrid region, in such neighbourhoods as the Fazenda of Santa Cruz and Campos. But the climate of these localities is totally unfit for European labour, as the Savoyard victims at Belem and the Swiss graves at Macucu might have taught the Brazilians, had they wished to learn. Between good soil and bad climate, bad soil and fair climate, the choice too often lies.

But there was a monster ravaging Rio de Janeiro, when the unfortunate British colonists returned from Cananea the other day, which has still less the freedom of the tropics—a python born of the union of refuse with the soft sea wind, springing into fearful activity just where her humid breath kisses his stagnant hiding-places. The yellow fever is altogether unknown over a vast extent of tropical America. The Pacific coast is, with some exceptions, exempt from it; and in Central America generally, unless it be at the Atlantic part of Greytown, this loathsome scourge is unheard of. It is perhaps no worse than some of our European forms of the family— certainly not than typhus. Unlike the latter, it leaves no results, while it is far more expeditious in making up its mind—a characteristic which may, however, be variously appreciated. Nor is it by any means so fatal as supposed, when promptly treated; and one doctor I knew had, in 1871, a merely nominal percentage of casualties.* Finally,

---

* I see in my journal, 1870, that of 300 cases admitted to the Sauda Hospital in January of that year, 82 died.

it is not contagious. Still, when the atmosphere is propitious and the cases multiply, it is a grim plague, and a bad inference against the climate; and the more so that it seems to infuse its working into the entire community.

> "For over all there came a kind of fear,
> A sense of mystery the spirit daunted,
> And spoke as plain as whisper in the ear,
> The place is haunted."

Whether it be panic, or more probably some real action on the system, the spell acts on all men, sound and sick, mostly intensifying, exaggerating their dispositions and intoxicating their spirits. All maladies and ailments then end in yellow Jack; and it would seem, not so much as if now and then an individual of the society had the fever, but rather as if the fever had the whole community—as the spider has the fly it has drugged, the owl the mouse its dreamy eyes have marked. Whether the dainties are eventually devoured is another question; but this year the vomito seems to be dispatching an unpleasant proportion. Instead of 20 deaths a day recorded in Rio in 1870, I see now from the papers as many as 40 per diem, representing perhaps 100 or 150 fresh cases in the twenty-four hours. The seeds of the disease appear to have been in the country for twenty to twenty-two years. It was preceded by a fever known as the polka fever, being contemporaneous with the first introduction of that dance.

It certainly would seem at present to be endemic, although there was a pause in its periodical return before 1869. When not very rife, it usually selects its victims from new comers, then Europeans generally, and only when the appetite has been sharpened by eating, preys upon natives or coloured humanity—niggers being almost exempt. This fine discrimination may account for the comparative nonchalance with which the Flumineuses, as they style themselves, continue to regard the periodical visitations of a scourge the control of which lies, after all, so much within their power. Those who have seen carcases floating in the canal, a dead mule lying weeks by the principal roadside; who have watched the hideous scenes of blood and vultures at Saŏ Christovâo, or the tideless shallows dancing for ever the self-same refuse on the shore; who remember water at 1s. 6d. a tiny barrel, in the capital, while ancient intrigue still disputed what company, of the many offering, should be allowed to confer this blessed necessity upon the town; who are haunted by these and such like reminiscences of the half-drained city in the marsh, can think it no wonder if the vomito cling to and nestle in the spot. Now the German consul, to-morrow the English, have three crewless vessels on their hands; now a few score emigrants have passed from their ship to the fine hospital, and from the hospital to a better place;—such things are injurious to commerce, and bad enough; but though they call forth the pleasant ticklings of benevolence, they do not raise wheals like fear. I remember talking of the yellow fever to a cultivated and distinguished native as we steamed one day across the sunny bay. "Getting bad?" said I. "Oh no," said he. "Twenty cases a-day, though!" "All foreigners," said he. This was instructive enough on the subject of "points of view." But I went on :—

"Beg your pardon, but there are now cases of Brazilians," mentioning such and such a one.

"From the interior and from other provinces" (no Flumineuses), calmly rejoined the large-minded patriot.

Here we are landed with the cod-fish and the calves again. It is all point of view; and some such consideration may explain the fact that even Saõ Fidelis, on the Parahyba, where the soil is fertile, but the climate stifling beyond anything in the province, has lately been suggested as a good centre for colonization.

Since the day when Galvani's dead frog lay quivering on the table, we have made considerable progress in observing the wide and varied range of action of a mode of force whose workings formerly counted among the instances of the supernatural, or passed altogether unheeded. Though the arcana of this mysterious power are still unpenetrated, no one now ignores its constant effective action on the human frame; its close connection with nervous energy, muscular power, and all states of health and disease. Such being the close connection between electricity and life, the electrical conditions of a country must be one of the most important elements in estimating its climate. Subject, no doubt, to constant change and fluctuation, both from the seasons and from causes of slower and of wider action, there is, nevertheless, often sufficient permanence in these conditions in various places to enable them to be considered as part of the basis of any judgment pronounced on climate. These conditions in Rio de Janeiro are those that precede a storm. In fact, the country has been, electrically speaking, waiting for a thunderstorm for some years past. Formerly these storms, of which there is so much need, came daily with such regularity that men made appointments by them, as they would by the movements of the sun. Some years ago this regularity ceased, and the storms became rare, a state of things which reached tension-point before the outbreak of the fever, in 1869–70. It was clear enough to many people that the health of the province and the storms were intimately related; as to the vigour of the individual, horse-flies are the only creatures to whom the final outburst of thunder and lightning brings no resurrection. From the electrical peculiarities of the climate, then, the European will have much to suffer in many parts of Brazil.

I do not pretend to know anything about ozone—whether it be a form of oxygen in which the atoms are peculiarly grouped, or what; but I believe, like my betters, in its important hygienic value. Well, the first thing I heard of ozone in Brazil was from the captain of the mail steamer, who informed me simply, that on the southern coast, near Rio, it did not exist. Ozone papers, moreover, have, as I have been informed, never detected but the smallest quantity of that invigorating combination in the air.

But unless this should smack too much of meteorological alchemy, I will finish up with one fact, showing that there are spots in Brazil which, for tropical localities, are peculiarly unfortunate. By far the chief mortality of Rio de Janeiro is from consumption.

Meanwhile, let it not be understood that I would include half a continent in one predicate, or class the Brazilian climate with the lethal ones of earth. It has its good sides and its bad, and territories under the prevailing influences of either; but it is not such but what it behoves Brazilians, especially colonization agents, to retain their modesty of expression; and unless from a vegetable or insect point of view, it must not be compared with that of Europe, nor, what is here more immediately to the purpose, with that of more favoured tropical districts.

An agriculturist runs the risk of suffering in one

of three ways from this climate; either from terrible droughts of long continuance; from frost on his plantations, if he lives in the highlands, or from permanently diminished energies for work, if he inhabit the warm lowlands. There are undoubtedly districts in which these inconveniences are reduced to a minimum, or wanting altogether; but that will be a lucky colony for which such a site is selected, with good soil and neighbouring port or market into the bargain!

How such a damp climate as has been described can suffer from drought may appear strange; it is, however, easily intelligible. Such a vast empire as Brazil is a little universe; what applies to the coast land is no longer true of the high plateaux of the interior, where the breezes arrive drained of their moisture; while the climate of the northern and southern provinces can rarely be included in one bracket.

The burning sun and high temperature of the tropical districts makes, moreover, an exceptionably long cessation of rain, even in the usualld humid regions, more fatally pernicious than it would be in cooler lands, though it may not affect the question of the general moisture of the climate. One or two frosts a year are sufficient, as we know, to exclude certain productions altogether from many countries, no matter how favourable to their development the remaining time may be. Serious droughts, however rare, are equally pernicious to many forms of culture, and are the bane of such provinces as Rio Grande do Norte, Piauhy, Pernambuco, Sergipe Goyaz, Ceará and Matto-Grozo, being more frequent in some than others, and mostly confined to the interior regions of those which border on the sea. Even Rio de Janeiro has cried aloud for water; and in 1869 the people of Saõ Paolo were starving on that account, and provisions had to be dispatched to them from Rio.

As to fertile land there is undoubtedly a good deal in Brazil, mostly, when not appropriated, grown over with dense forest; but there are also vast districts of fern (Pteris aquilina, Mertensia dichotoma) and of coarse rough grass—infallible indications of barrenness and poverty of soil, wide tracts of sand supporting only the columnar cactus and contorted bushes, broad wastes of quartz rock defying even these pioneers of vegetation.

Perhaps the commonest soil, and that which colonists mostly come in contact with, is that derived from the gneiss or granite rock, with its conical hills of all sizes, and its accompanying pasty clays and drifts. It forms the greatest part of the province of Rio de Janeiro and a vast portion of Brazil, an analogous red drift having been found by Agassiz on the shores of the Amazons and by Darwin on the Plate. Such a formation is likely to produce a soil of, on the whole, far from startling fertility.

According to the varying proportions of the constituents of that most uncertain rock, and its mechanical condition, whether as solid stone, soft yielding masses, or as triturated paste, it will include all limits between the desert and the garden. The latter quality, under the name of "barro vermelho," is highly esteemed, has been much sought after, and in many places converted into the most flourishing native estates of the Empire. The former kinds constitute a large part of the starved highlands on which the colonies of Petropolis, Juiz da Fora, and Theresopolis were founded.

There is plenty of land in Brazil, on which anybody may settle for the smallest consideration, just as there are scores of rivers in which anyone is free to wash for diamonds. Good land, however, in convenient neighbourhoods and streams which roll octohedral crystals, are not in quest since yesterday alone, nor open to the first comer. The best soils in all localities have long ago been "viewed," and where it was possible to bring them into tolerable communication with a market, appropriated, if not cultivated. Round the large capitals and towns are often immense areas of land which the owners do not cultivate, but which are not on that account to be had at a moderate figure, for their drone-like proprietors, often enough, will not part with them. We have already referred, in the instance of Sta Isabel, to the cramping effects of this dog-in-the-manger disposition. Let a Brazilian, the Director of the Emigration Society, Senhor Tavares Bastos, now speak a word on the subject:—

"One of the greatest obstacles to spontaneous emigration consists in the fact of a vast extent of the best land, and that which is situated in the vicinity of markets and roads, being in the possession of large landowners. This fatal consequence of the unintelligent system of grants, followed without discrimination by the metropolitan Government, is, in addition to the above evil, likewise a bar to the development of free labour in the country."

Such are the fetters to her natural development which still hang on Brazil as heirlooms of the colonial days. Mr. Hermann Haupt speaks thus on the same subject:—

"The Portuguese system bequeathed to the Empire a deplorable state of things with regard to the land. All that gave promise in more or less distant days of wealth, had been disposed of to private persons whether by gift or sale. The nation thus found itself bereft of Crown lands in those situations of the various provinces in which they were most needed. The coast provinces no longer possess any, and only in the interior, and in distant provinces of lesser importance, are fertile and extensive State lands still to be found."

It is startling to find tenants on the edge of virgin woods holding by the feudal payment of ground-rent, but rich is the "foro" which Brazilian Marquesses of Carabas receive in exchange for their perpetual leases. The gifts of principalities, the wasteful system of agriculture on a large scale, the employment of slave labour, the prejudice against foreigners, and the impossibility of providing them with lands, are all of a piece, and hang together. For long no more such gifts of one or two hundred square miles have been made; but Brazilians who have the best information, through their scouts, continued and continue to pounce upon each rare discovery of a really fertile nook, and buy up districts equalling a parish or a county, without any corresponding obligation to cultivate them. Thus we have such vast latifundists as the Baron das tres Barras and the Clemente Pintos, and it were well indeed for Brazil if all her territorial magnates were cast of the same metal as these latter. But the descendants of the old grantees are not all so enlightened, nor is any qualification necessary for the possession of a kingdom in Brazil. When the lands were brought into cultivation, it was on a system which in its wild destruction resembled the forest fires with which it commenced; ever consuming and advancing with only a desert in its rear. Virgin woods were burnt down; the virgin soil planted, exhausted, and abandoned; when, locust-like, the Fazendeiro, and his band of blacks, passed on to fresh destruction, reckless of the future climate and agricultural prospects of the country thus laid waste. "Après moi le déluge," was the ruling maxim in this heedless hurry to grow rich. And the deluge came, indeed, very literally over large areas where the fire had passed before, the deluge of the tropic rains sweeping bald the unprotected hill tops, and washing their last rests of humus to the river beds.

It is a singular fact, noticed to me by more than one person of experience in Brazil, that the climate of the serra has been affected by the destruction of forests in a way exactly the reverse of what we expect in Europe, the rains having increased, the cold diminished. This is also the reverse of what could be wished in Brazil, and accompanied furthermore by a great augmentation of the denuding and devastating power of the rains.

Thus, then, not only have a great proportion of the available lands been taken, but taken and destroyed; while we cannot suppose that it is to the exhausted tracks of thin capoeira (second growth) that the Empire's panegyrists make appeal.

Slaves do not live for ever, nor would the slave-trade last for ever; hay had to be made while the sun shone; and surely it was shining with an African to be got for 10*l.*! "lots more where he came from," and the coast still free. The work, the workman, and the scale of operations were all matched; what small proprietor, or free settler, could compete with such an agricultural stampede?

but the line of yet unpillaged soil recedes yet ever farther from the coast, the slaves are now dying, the traffic stopped, the institution mined, and the days of such latifundists and locust farmers at an end. The nation will soon, indeed, have leisure and motives for turning its attention once more to the desert on which this desolation has passed; but it will be generations before the land recovers a fair proportion of its pristine virtue.

It has been proposed to grapple with this state of things by expropriation laws, replacing the State in possession of some of the large areas which reckless colonial policy formerly bestowed on private persons; and also, in like manner, to confer on the central authority, in consideration for a proper indemnity, the control and ownership of extensive public lands still held by many of the provinces. Another caustic remedy proposed is a land-tax, which would compel the owners to cultivate or quit. It is easy to conceive the serried opposition likely to be arrayed against such surgical reforms, until such times, at least, as the disease shall have reached its acutest phase. Against the latter measure the Brazilian Fazendeiro—who is now well into a bog which none but the sturdiest can hope to wade through—may reasonably urge a good deal. All his instruments of production are continually rising in price; his distance from the market has increased; competition in his principal staple, coffee, is likely to augment; and he has already to bear the burden not only of a considerable provincial and imperial tax on his produce, but of what is equivalent to a tax on his drove of mules, for the imperial dues are levied *ad valorem* on the market price *in the port*. Under the present circumstances, very many of the class are more or less deeply indebted, and not even the late depreciation of the currency enabled them to clear themselves. Put an additional burden in the shape of a land-tax upon them, and will they ever get out of the bog, some of the most quaggy portions of which lie still before them? If such a tax were introduced at all, it should be as a tax on *non-cultivation*, applied in inverse ratio to the production, the uncleared wilderness, after so many years' possession, paying the most; the thriving fazenda a mere nominal sum. But we are not now concerned with remedies for this diseased state of things, having here only the more invidious task of registering the presence of the malady, as one largely affecting the question of colonization.

The romantic reputation of Brazil has profited by her propinquity to Europe, from which it is directly reached by sea. It has thus been for many Europeans who have visited that country, the first and often also the last glimpse of tropic magnificence. Now, though I would be the last to disparage the grandeur, colour, and luxuriance of that beautiful land, I must confess that older travellers, accustomed to note things closely, and coming from other regions of the American tropics which I am acquainted with, to Rio de Janeiro, would certainly be *struck* with the vegetation; but it would be rather with the *absence* of a certain wild luxuriance, with the want of giant forms. Here the fact that he was contemplating the second growth of an exhausted soil; there, the bleak situation on the sierra might explain, but would not alter, the case; at times he would plunge into a rich gorge, and console himself with admiring some huge iron-tree, or the spreading crowns of half a dozen Jequetivá; there, again, he might come across the lofty Re do Matto, king of the woods, or the swollen carcase of a Bombax. But in all this he would see little but what torrid sun and water could work out of a thin soil, and the memory of the Ceibas, Taxodiums, &c., of his former travels would come back like recollections of another race. In a word, such provinces as Rio de Janeiro certainly produce a very great variety of beautiful woods, but the growth of the trees, though striking to an European, is not, as a rule, luxuriant for the tropics, nor is the size attained remarkable. Though it occasionally happened, it was rare that I came, in my constant raids through virgin wood, across a tree of greater girth than three times my extended arms, at 4 or 5 feet from the ground, a fine size in a Swiss pine.

Most larger trees are show-trees. It has been said in the usual hyperbolical style of the so-called friends of Brazil, that you need but scratch the surface of the earth and a crop will come up. Scratching the red crumbling gneiss is not, however, on the whole, to be recommended. The next rain may lay bare a stonier layer. I found during some little experience, which may, however, I believe, be fairly taken as typical at least of the usual upland slopes, that to get grass for a horse or cow a goodly plastering with manure is absolutely necessary, and that in all but the coolest or most fertile neighbourhoods, each plant of grass *had to be planted by hand.* The grass thus treated, the Capim d'Angola, is fortunately more luxuriant when started than that of European hay-fields; but it must be weeded, hoed, and manured continually, or it would soon disappear under scrub and fern.*

Tried again by comparison with other countries, we do not find that the productions of Brazil make up in quality any shortcoming in quantity. The coffee of Brazil, though better than its reputation, ranks, with certain unimportant exceptions, very

---

* Of the usual tropic plagues Brazil has her share, like other lands. It is not necessary to catalogue them here, the more so as they are well known. But as the prophets of colonization are hardly as modest as they might be, I annex this note of the fellest. Droughts, floods, fires, birds, ants, such as the fearful Saüba (Atta Cephalotes), caterpillars, monkeys, and, lastly, what affects agriculture by incapacitating the husbandman, numerous poisonous snakes. Of the latter I saw more in Brazil than I have come across elsewhere in the tropics.

low in the market. It fetches a lower price, and may consequently be presumed inferior to that of Ceylon, Mocha, Java, the West Indies, Central America, and most other countries; and yet coffee is the plant of all others to thrive in light soil and hill lands.

Another tropical staple whose virtue will depend on certain subtle principles to be elaborated from the soil is the material of chocolate, the fruit of Theobroma cacao. This tree is extensively cultivated in the northern provinces; but here, again, while the cacao of Soconusco, in Guatemala, was reserved for the tables of kings, and very superior kinds are produced in Caraccas, and other old Spanish colonies, that of Brazil is of inferior quality, whence, no doubt, the different reputation in Europe of Spanish and Portuguese chocolate.

Again, Bahia produces very fair tobacco; but the general quality of the crop raised in Brazil is below that of many tropical lands, both in delicacy and potency of flavour and in freedom from attacks of insects while in store.

The real secret of Brazil as a field of enterprise is the stability of the Government and the peaceful, inoffensive character of the Portuguese race, not the peculiar virtues of her soil nor the exceptional alchemy of her sunlight.

Were climate and fertility all that had to be considered, there are portions of Central America known to me which must, I believe, be pronounced to be greatly superior. The trees are larger, the soil more fertile, and the coffee, cacao, and tobacco superior; while the list of other productions includes almost every staple of the tropics, indigo, sarsaparilla, cochineal, vanilla, balsams, india-rubber, not to mention mineral wealth, which may yet be found to rival that of Minas. Beautiful timber abounds in both countries; but beautiful timber is not always useful, being hard and heavy, and often growing sporadically. Thus Brazil is compelled to import large quantities of deal from rimy Norway, while the hills of Central America, on the other hand, are dark with forests of gigantic pines. But through pines and palms alike of that unfortunate land comes ever and anon on the soft wind the harsh sound of "muera" this one, or "muera" that one, and so the beautiful siren still remains eclipsed by her far more homely but more honest rival.

Giving, then, this great Lusitanian empire its just due, while divesting it of the paint, padding, and perfume with which narrow-minded and mostly interested panegyrists have disguised it, we come to the question, Is there anything transcendent in the soil or climate which, even *cæteris paribus*, should be held sufficient to allure Englishmen from their homes, or divert them, when bent on wandering, from British colonies both within and without the tropics?

If not, in what shall we hope to find the solid

advantages with which to justify the rash experiment? It is not in affinity of race; no Brazilian will attempt to class the Saxon or the Celt with the Portuguese, the negro, or the Puri. It is not in the mutual comprehension and reciprocal suitability of opposite or complementary characters; although Brazilians may, as a rule, understand Englishmen and their institutions somewhat better than Senador Junqueira, who, during my stay in Rio, rose in his place in Cortes and said, "The English have in their legislation absurdities not in that of Brazil; for example, the provision which authorizes a husband to take his wife to a market, and sell her there." Englishmen in their turn often enter into the workings of the Brazilian mind no better than a batch of British colonists I saw in Rio, entered into the reiterated offers of the Brazilian Government to remove them to any colony which they liked of a number proposed, or to secure them work elsewhere, coupled, however, with the refusal to pay certain accounts which the Englishmen presented for work done in the colony they had come from. It was alleged, with some reason, that the books of the colony having been destroyed, the Government had no means of checking these accounts. But it was a point of view John Bull could not see at all. He had "cut down their woods for them, and was willing to do it again, but paid he must be before he budged anywhere else."

It were already a bad enough business to plant artichokes with lilies, or cage the lammergier with macaws; but with man, race, besides the vegetable life and animal, means the hidden framework on which delicate tissues of custom, character, and morals are extended, including everything from food to faith. On the former we will not dwell, though the bread and beef eating Englishman would content himself quite otherwise than the German, on bananas, beans, and *carne secca*. But from the latter, with the intellectual bent and moral sense, hangs the important meshwork of the law and all its stays of custom.

Brazil is not bigoted, but the Roman Catholic faith is the religion of the land, and as such ultramontanism, tradition, and superstitious indifferentism will sustain it for some time to come. The Protestant emigrant, meanwhile, will enjoy full freedom of conscience, little affected by the fact that his chapel bell cannot be rung, and that the functions of senator and deputy are inhibited to him. As long as the colony remains compacted in its clearing, a little *imperium in imperio*, he will feel no isolation. He may even separate from the nucleus and travel the country, like a stone in a horse's foot, without being distressed by any approach to religious zeal in those he meets. It is only when induced to strive after closer assimilation than such a stone, when he would drive roots and suck nourishment, when he would influence at least the provincial and municipal councils of his adopted land,—only then will the "heretico" feel his alienation and the limits of religious tolerance.

Or the revelation may come upon him in the sacred relations of the family, in a land where the want of civil marriage reduces Protestant wedded life to a legalized concubinage. We will hope he has arrived married, so that he may be secure from making the experience in his person. Being an Englishman, however, his daughters will be quite white, and being quite white, they will, in the eyes of young Brazilians, be beauties. A mixed marriage takes place. The consent of the bishop, to begin with, costs $32—about 3*l.* 5*s.*—and, as well as the celebration of the marriage, is conditional on an oath being taken by the parties that all the children will be brought up as Catholics. If such demands are to be made by the Catholics in England, as certain late occurrences might alarm one into supposing, English Protestant fathers will know what to do; but an emigrant to a Catholic country may have but the only alternative of condemning his children to perpetual celibacy, his family to extinction. Besides, the marriage, or worse, may, and probably will, take place anyhow, though he shut up his Danaë in a tower of bronze.

To such mixed unions as secure the progeny to the Church, the bishops will naturally make no objections. But there are other cases arisen out of this incongruous state of things which are among the grossest scandals of the kind in Christendom. The colonist may arrive as a bachelor, and marry in the country. Supposing he is duly married to another Protestant by the clergyman of the colony, his marriage will, according to the late law, of September 1861, and the subsequent regulations of April, 1863, be duly recognized as valid for all civil purposes. But one of the parties may subsequently be won over to the Catholic faith, and then comes the possibility of the other being made the victim of an unjust and immoral decision, such as startled all Rio, in 18... To give somebody his due, I do not think a second edition of that insult to humanity is likely to be tried in Brazil; and the late judgment of the Bishop of Saö Paolo, in a somewhat similar case, shows that the enlightened spirit of the Church condemns it. Still, it was not till 1861-63 that the Protestant got tolerable security for his marriage at all, by the establishment of the competency of the civil tribunals to decide on thèm; and by the due legalization of marriages by Protestant pastors, which guaranteed him from moral obliquity in high places. Now for the case.

A Protestant Swiss woman, wife of a Protestant, duly married at the altar, went over to the Roman Catholic religion. The worthiness of the motives of this change has been emphatically denied; and certainly the immediate results of the conversion gave fair grounds for the denial. The priesthood of the convert's new Church was soon called upon to sanction and bless her union with a Catholic. The question being referred to the authorities of the bishopric of Rio de Janeiro, they found it conformable to their instincts of purity and the spirit of their Church to decide in favour of the adulterous tie, on the ground, it appears, that a disparity of faith—"cultus disparitas"—reduced the previous *bonâ fide* marriage with a Protestant to concubinage. This decision created almost universal indignation at the time; but I am not aware that it was ever rescinded.

A subsequent judgment, rendered, in 1862, by the more enlightened bishopric of Saŏ Paolo, redeemed the honour at the price of the consistency of the Church.

Two Swiss Protestants had been duly married,* had lived together as man and wife, and had two children. According to the law of 1861, above cited, this marriage would seem to have been perfectly valid and in due form. But it is provided by the law that no marriage shall be held valid to which there are such impediments as would invalidate a Catholic marriage. It appears, furthermore, that, according to the canonical law received in the

---

* Whether only civilly, or civilly with some religious ceremony, is not quite clear.

empire, disparity of religious belief—" cultus disparitas "—is such an impediment.* Now, it happened that Wilhelm Blathner took it into his head that he preferred a Brazilian woman to his countrywoman and wedded spouse. Wilhelm Blathner accordingly, as a first step, had himself admitted into the bosom of the Catholic Church. He next applied for an injunction to be furnished from the Governador do Bispado of the province, for the celebration of his nuptials with his Catholic bride. To this application he eventually received an answer which must have made him wince—pronouncing him still bound by the tie contracted as a " heretic," forbidding him altogether fresh nuptials, urging him to work out the conversion of his Swiss wife, impressing on him the education of his children in the true religion, and finishing with a moral couched in the brevity of eloquence—" pague as custas," let him pay the costs. This document is signed Joachim Manoel Gonzalves de Andrade—to whom be all honour.

The last part of this decision calls upon the couple to " educate their children in the one true religion, as *they had already promised to do while in the state of heretics.*" Does this mean that such a promise had been extracte from two Protestants at the

---

* Mixed marriages are, no doubt, considered by the Church as evil in themselves; but to be allowed for special purposes, one such purpose being proselytism. Hence the facility at present granted for their celebration.

time of drawing up the marriage act? Even the benefit of civil marriage, coupled with such an obligation, would be a farce.

Of a verity one would have thought that a fierce sun, African and Indian blood, a celibate caste, and inhuman solitudes, were sufficient impulse to concubinage and free love, without a state of law such as the above cases betray.

Marriage suggests, or at least produces children, and children will sooner or later make the colonist's family acquainted with other laws of the empire, for which, in his stolidity, he will probably be little prepared. These are the laws of succession and inheritance. If he has married a wife without making a contract,—and a contract he is not likely to have made,—and if this wife dies before him, he will be startled by learning that with the dissolution of the partnership in this manner, he loses his rights over one-half of his own hard-earned property, which becomes vested in the children. Nay, in default of the latter, he may be even more grievously disconcerted by an intimation on the part of his wife's relations, advancing on their own account a claim to a like amount—a demand in which the law will give them an unqualified support. He is not likely to marry many successive times under these circumstances, but it is easy to picture his ultimate position and that of his heirs by his last wife if so be he did!

If the shock of this discovery be too much for him, and he follow his wife to the grave, his children will have an opportunity of making acquaintance with another branch of Brazilian law, and, what will touch them closer, with the administration thereof. I allude to the provisions respecting the guardianship of orphans.

I have heard much of the integrity of the court invested with this charge in Rio de Janeiro, and have even heard Englishmen aver that they would rather have its tutorship than that of their own consuls. I doubt if anything of importance can be advanced against its written precepts. But there are places in the empire in reaching which a letter grows yellow, where it seems indeed for those who wait for justice, that " the heaven is high and the Emperor far," and where all depends on the character and integrity of subordinate functionaries. That the incorruptible probity of these latter is not always sufficiently rigid to guarantee the fate and fortune of alien infants is too well known to serious Brazilians. But if anyone will read the horrible fate of two girls, the orphan children of a German colonist, related by Tschudi,* it will give him a crying instance of what enormities may happen without the authorities having even a chance of prevention.

Not only the fate of orphans, but all matters of succession to the property of a dead colonist, are of

* " Journey through Brazil," visit to the Province of Espirito Santo.

course, by right, in the hands of the local authorities, subject alike to Brazilian law and Brazilian loitering. In Petropolis, the tact of the late German consul had created a happy exception; by an affable, intelligent understanding with the native officials, based on a knowledge of character, he kept the practical management of most cases of succession among his countrymen in his own hands. The authorities were of course called upon to validate all formalities, but the wills were written in German, and consequently Greek to Brazilian eyes. The fact is mainly important as showing the weight attached, both by the consul and his clients, to the intervention of some non-native element in order to secure prompt and certain liquidation of testamentary business. It has taken the Brazilian authorities, in one case, as much as eight years to wind up the affairs of a dead Englishman.

It has been often and justly remarked that a very imperfect code promptly administered with impartiality and uniformity, is better than very superior legislation applied by vacillating and dilatory hands. It is not alone in cases of inheritance that the foreigner will meet with opportunities of verifying the truth of this statement in Brazil. Delays, amounting at times to a denial of justice, are only too common both in criminal and civil causes. Brazilians are well acquainted through the columns of their own publications with the case of George

Adolphus Stolze, a German, established in the province of Bahia, whose cause was espoused by the Sociedade International de Immigração, and who is spoken of in reports of that society as "atrociously persecuted, ill-treated, and injured by the authorities of the backwoods (Sertoes) of Bahia, notwithstanding that his cause was, and was acknowledged by other authorities to be, most just." But the efforts of the society appear to have been as vain as those of Stolze himself on his arrival in Rio. For years he remained without reparation, and, for all I know to the contrary, remains still in the same predicament.

A lawyer of the capital told me once that he had been more than a year endeavouring to recover the small sum of 3*l*. for a client. A case came under my notice of an immigrant kept nearly three months in prison on a charge of threatening, and then dismissed for want of evidence; of an Englishman charged with assault, and only brought to trial after ten months; of another committed on suspicion of robbery, and not brought to trial after nine months. A whole crew was committed for murder of their captain in March, 1869, first tried in December, 1869, and acquitted; tried again on judge's appeal, May, 1870, and all condemned to various punishments with the exception of the man who had actually struck the blow, who was acquitted. Finally they were tried on their own appeal, June,

1870, and once more all acquitted. These men were consequently nine months in obtaining a trial, a year and three months in obtaining a final verdict!!

Some cases require to be indicated to show that the above views are no results of idle prejudice; but as it is very far from my intention to lay a formal indictment against a nation, there is no need to be more communicative and explicit. Those who require further corroboration will find it in the speeches of Brazilian senators and deputies, in the archives of consuls, and in the honest avowals of all Brazilians, who, as true lovers of their country, would not,

> "Like to the owner of a foul disease,
> To keep it from disclosing, let it feed
> Upon the pith of life."

The administration of justice, like many other institutions of the country, is tainted with the virus of petty personal politics, and perverted by good fellowship. Blood is stronger than water—$\chi\epsilon\iota\rho$ $\chi\epsilon\iota\rho\alpha$ $\nu\iota\pi\tau\epsilon\iota$, and to refuse to serve my cousin or my neighbour, by merely shutting an eye on occasions, at no expense to myself, would be unkind. Finally, mutual complacency becomes the rule, and the first would-be exception must simply be content with burnt fingers. It is in part owing to such local interdependence, and to that false sympathy for the criminal rather than the victim, common to periods of under and over civilization, that culprits, especially those guilty of blood-violence, so often escape. The amount of murder and assassination in the country, though considerable, has, however, I believe, been greatly exaggerated, and, considering the vast extent and other circumstances of the country, is remarkably small. It is, moreover, almost entirely confined to cases of personal vengeance; thus leaving the prudent foreigner in perfect safety. The Portuguese race are pre-eminently long-suffering and peaceful, and the wildest districts, out of reach of Indians, may be traversed with no more deadly weapon than a tooth-pick.

Partizan madness, dignified by the name of politics, is in all respects the bane of the empire, entering into almost every question of life, hampering the real interests of the country, metamorphosizing subordinate local officials into powerful agents of electioneering tyranny, falsifying appreciations of material questions, and wasting the energies while perverting the sense of provincial and municipal institutions. Thus the question of a road, of a school, a church, divides the municipality into rabid reds and whites; militia service becomes, in the hands of skilful officers, a powerful engine of political intimidation, enlistment answers the same purpose, and acts of arbitrary tyranny are committed, now on this side, now on that, for the benefit of unscrupulous string-pullers who have devoted themselves to the profession of representative. Up the country I heard strange complaints from Fazendeiros of the way in which their interests were often sacrificed from contemptible party motives. I once had the honour of being the guest of an old man who had made one or two beautiful estates out of the matto, with plantations, parks, and mills, such as are nowhere to be surpassed. Lounging through the languid air of the hottest season over the rich green slopes of his domain, which hung above the rushing river, and discussing everything, from the grass at our feet to the future of the empire, we came, in our discursive talk, upon the sore subject of the national representation. Speaking to the son of the house—while my companion sauntered on, chatting to the energetic, practical creator of the ordered fertility about us—I asked him whether it were not possible to organize some sound representation of the agricultural, that is, of the vital interests of the country, some Fazendeiro party of the right sort?

"Ah," said my companion, a cultivated man of European experience, "my father was once induced to offer himself as deputy, and to go in that capacity to Rio; but he came back determined never to waste his time by a repetition of the experiment, and with the conviction that the Cortes was a nest of parrots." Other landed proprietors of my acquaintance, who belong to the most enlightened, wealthy, and energetic under the Southern Cross, pay as much attention to politics as they do to the distant sound of tumbling surf which catches their ears on their periodical visits to the capital.

When Brazil first shook off the leading-strings of Portugal, when separatist sentiments still were strong, and old interests and prejudices, working in remote districts, threatened the disintegration of the empire and the desertion of individual provinces, there were men of no illiberal mind who saw the necessity of strengthening the hands of the central power. They therefore sanctioned, or even strove after, a political system which they now consider to have done its work, and to require modification in many particulars. As it is, the President of the province, the delegados and other agents of the police, even the provincial and municipal authorities elected under the influence of the former, nay, the recruiting serjeants and the officers of the national guard, are so many wheels in a vast centralized machinery, shrieking forth the jargon of elections, and busy with the nothingness of party strife. Thus the President of the province, possessed of autocratic power, and with unlimited influence for weal or woe; the man on whose appreciation, together with that of the assemblies, each new project of improvement, whether road or rail, navigation, emigration, or what not, depends —this officer, with functions so essentially remote from imperial politics, holds his appointment at the good pleasure of the Crown, that is, of each successive Government! With a right to dismiss all but superior magistrates, and with an army of police functionaries, known as delegados and sub-delegados, at command, he were a bad general, indeed, that could not ensure the campaign.

Still, every victory thus gained is a reverse to the true progress of the country. The very expression of that political opinion on which so much stress is laid, is falsified or constrained by open violence, the energies of the land are exhausted by a vampire, and the councils of her citizens blinded by miasma.

All this concerns the future of the country, and consequently the colonist a good deal. He may conceive how much that is written in letters of gold on the law-books of the nation, becomes under such a system worthless as falling leaves in the regions of its application. He may thus understand how it is that so much of crime remains unpunished, how much the innocent may suffer before formal acquittal, and how elastic are the meshes of the law. Take, for instance, the noble provision for gratuitous national education in § 33 of Art. 179 of the nation's charter—of what avail is it, where the holdings lie scattered leagues apart, and the local authorities ever snarl and bicker over liberal and conservative views of the way the wished-for road should run? Or consider the following account (taken by the 'Anglo-Brazilian Times' from the 'Liberal' of Alagoas, of September, 1870) of the proceedings of some police and gendarmes of that province sent out to arrest some comrades of the latter, who had missed a parade, and compare it with paragraph 7 of Art. 179 as to inviolability of domicile. " Beginning their work at midnight, they searched 25 houses from top to bottom, tied up and took away 17 men and youths of all ages, thrashed 9 or 10 men and boys, ill-treated sundry mothers and wives, damaged crops wantonly, stole a number of things, including a demijohn of rum from an old woman .... broke open a trunk, took the lace from a pillow, and threw the blessed rosary of a woman into the fire": or read the speech of Senator Pompeo in the assembly of the nation in the same year, when he called attention to the increasing number of crimes encouraged by the impunity, and sometimes even protection, accorded by local authorities. I am afraid his words made small impression on the Government, χειρ χειρα νίπτει—constituents compel.

When, in addition to these reflections, we recollect the institution of capangas or bravos, and the custom of sheltering even monster criminals from pursuit, we have the same school-boy picture of want of public morality and respect for the law, the same absence of a sense of personal individual responsibility to the tribunal of conscience, which keeps so many Southern and Catholic nations in swaddling-clothes. Sods want a deal of turning before the old bog flowers cease to come up. The contraband laws of the gold and diamond monopolies, the colonial system, the Indian raids, and the illegal slave-trade, will bear their quagmire fruit for long after the land is drained.

There is an institution in Brazil pre-eminently calculated to render the citizen autocratical, arbitrary, and unscrupulous, tyrannical and purblind—which, by facile pandering to vice, mines and corrodes the pith and marrow of the family, and perverts the principles on which it rests,—an institution stultifying religion, clogging the step of statesmanship, and, like a foul wind, baffling the flight of humanizing thought. This institution—founded, nurtured, and safeguarded by the State, sanctioned and utilized by the Church—is interesting to the emigrant, independently of all its other influences, from representing the incarnate degradation of labour.

Manual toil is branded and dishonoured in Brazil—the treason to humanity has had a retractive curse, and the hand that once smote the nigger, when called upon to save the country, falls blighted to the side. The Brazilian neither can nor will work; hence the still greater urgency than otherwise for obtaining a supply of those who will do so for him. To play the statesman, the deputy, the merchant, the speculator, the innkeeper, the huckster, the overseer, the skipper, the "camarade," the coachman, the boatman, the woodranger, or the angler, he is willing and often capable enough; but to anoint his palm and handle a spade, to hew, delve, or do any hard handiwork whatsoever, is against his stomach, whether physical or moral, and irksome to his spine.

In a growing community, where a horny palm and a handy fist should be the noblest distinction; the heavy foot from treading, the big thumb from twisting, and the thick lip from wetting the flax, the best dowry in a wife; men grow up as effete and helpless as in ancient Sybaris or Croton. To carry a pill-box or a peascod through the streets of Rio is to proclaim yourself a pariah; to walk with a carpet-bag or paper parcel, excommunication. I well remember the gauntlet of eyes fixed upon me in blank amazement each time I landed from the 'Petropolis' steamer, and walked bag in hand through the rank of greasy chapmen to the nearest tramway. Sometimes there was a touch of pity, but always the most profound astonishment at the menial tastes of one who seemed certainly quite as white and nearly as well-bred as themselves. I recollect a lad of fifteen or so, who used sometimes to sleep out at a house I occasionally visited, his family living some three or four miles away. As happens with improvident youth of all nations, his luggage often consisted of a hairbrush and a collar, with, may be, a toothbrush to boot. Such a parcel slips easily into a pocket; but the poor boy was the creole of a slave land, born under the ban, so he must needs go home unburdened, and send a slave trotting the long distance to bring back his things. This occurred over and over again, and yet we are told labour is scarce in such a country!

The choice on the large estates of the province of Rio de Janeiro, which could formerly count on an importation of from 20,000 to 30,000 blacks per annum, has not hitherto been between slave and free labour, but between the nigger and nothing. For not only has the number of hands introduced as immigrants remained as a rule at half that of the annual slave supply of former years, but the material thus obtained is so unsuited to the purposes of the great Fazendeiros, that, without a complete subversion of the present system, it could hardly be made to pay. As an auxiliary for agriculture on the old scale its value is little higher; since it is almost as impracticable to supplement slave labour with free as oil with water. The Parceria colonies, though a failure, were in so far right, as they were rather a complete substitution of the one kind of labour for the other—white for black—than an attempt to work them in the same yoke. But (though a long lease on good terms and under favourable circumstances might sometimes content the colonist) it is, as a rule, his *own* fig-tree that the emigrant desires to sit under, not the banana of another, no matter how full of fruit. The union of labour with possession, by the institution of small properties worked by the owners, would seem the best chance left of rehabilitating labour. Anyhow, whether the change come about by sale, rents, enfiteusis,* or what, there are many signs indicating that the days of the vast sugar and coffee plantations on the old scale are numbered. In some cases, where the soil is much exhausted, their place will probably be taken by cattle runs and parks, requiring few hands, and suiting the Brazilian indole; in others, they must, it would seem, in time be broken up into smaller holdings, having their necessary machinery in common in some central locality, just as is the case in the olive districts of parts of Italy, the cheese-farming in Switzerland, and the cane-growing of certain portions of Brazil. Meanwhile we may understand how, as things now are, several score emigrants may be found occasionally in Rio with anything but the aspect of the right thing in the right place; one-half of the community will have nothing to do with them, while with the other they will have nothing to do.

One of the first requisites, then, for a wholesome immigration on a right footing, is that the honour of labour should be re-established; and this can only fully happen after slavery has been for some time totally abolished. But meanwhile the peculiar institution directly affects labour by the diminution of its proper remuneration. This is practically the case

* Permanent leases, paying a fixed quit-rent.

with regard to the spontaneous emigration of those classes, such as mechanics, artizans, and skilled labourers, which first finding a footing in large towns, would otherwise eventually spread over the country, or found families of children who did. But the hire of these classes, independently of the low purchasing power of money, and the other inconveniences existing in Brazil, is not high enough to induce the exportation of men who, at the present day in Europe, hold the ball of fortune in their hands. The reason of this must, I think, be in great measure sought in the one and a-half to one and three-quarter millions of slaves in the empire, or more especially in that portion of this huge total which is held in ports and cities. In Rio de Janeiro, in 1870, every fifth man was a slave.

Men not only use this species of cattle themselves, but they let it out to others, and consequently a considerable portion of the 50,092 slaves of the capital are always to be had at rates of wages kept at a comparatively low figure by the competition of the owners. The African, if confined to one kind of work, not only often makes an excellent subordinate artizan, but may even be trusted, when the sphere of action is capable of definite demarcation, with the duties of master-workman. Thus it is that the black is hired out right and left, here to a gas company, there to a manufacturer, here as porter, there as pedlar, now to mend my lady's dresses, now to mend the road. Few handicrafts have not their nigger adepts, who may be found from the smithy to the pastrycook's.

When human beings come into the markets, whether of Europe or America, besides the simple rules of supply and demand, there comes the question of the minimum for which they *can* live, and for which they *will* work. Now, when our hungry European, keen from the sea-air, attempts to make his terms, he will find he has to reckon with a competitor that can live on quite other food than he, and that his *will* to work for it is effectively galvanized by a cat and palmatorio in the background. Well if he be not startled on the morning of his landing by some such advertisements as the following:—

"To be sold beyond the limits of the municipality of the Court, a little mulatto 15 years old, who has commenced the trade of carpenter, and is also a good house servant. Further particulars, Rua Direita, No. 8, at the end of the 2nd storey."

"To be sold a negress, eleven years of age, very pretty and perfect, also a black lad who can cook, &c., &c. Na Rua do Principe dos Cajueiros, No. 20." Or, again:—

"For sale, a mare and three months' foal, Minas race; the property of an Englishman returning home, who is particularly anxious to find a good home for them."

No! What am I thinking of, I took the wrong

paragraph. This is the right one. "To let" . . .
No! It had better remain in original:—
"Alugase uma ama de leite, moça sadia e com leite de mez—na Rua do Nuncio, No. 20A, &c."*

Some such influences as the above are necessary to account for daily wages of only from 3s. to 5s. for engineers; 2s. to 3s. for blacksmiths; 3s. to 4s. for carpenters; 2s. 6d. to 4s. for roadmakers and navvies; or from 4s. to 7s. to mechanics in the "Uniao e Industria's" workshops at Juiz da Fora; while I found an Italian Swiss carpenter up the country, a good workman, and apparently in his line a sort of mainstay of the estate, working for about 3s. 2d. a day and his food.† A blacksmith in England earns at present from 5s.; a navvy, 4s.; an engineer, 6s. 9d.; a carpenter, 6s. 9d.; a superior mechanic, 7s. In Germany, in many cases, wages are now very high, having risen 40 to 50 per cent. in most trades since 1865. Thus we have, in Wurtemberg, wages of adults ranging from 1s. 6d. to 2s. 11d. in most factories, though going as high as 4s. 2d. in some; and in some trades much higher rates—as printers, 4s. 2d.; carpenters, 2s. 6d. in the country, 3s. 6d. in Stuttgart; smiths, 2s. 3d. in the country, 2s. 11d. in Stuttgart; masons, 3s. 8d.; and

---

* Three of these advertisements, including the Portuguese one, are cut from the daily papers.
† See Secretary's Report for 1870. For information respecting navvies, &c., I am indebted to the kindness of Mr. Morritt.

quarrymen as much at times as 8s. 4d.! In Prussia we find (Mr. Petre's Report) many classes of labourers receiving from 2s. to 3s. a day, in 1870; in Paris, in 1869, a blacksmith gaining from 4s. to 6s. 4¾d.; a brickmaker, from 2s. 9½d. to 4s. 9½d.; a carpenter, 4s. 9½d.; joiners and masons, over 4s.; quarrymen, from 2s. 9d. to 4s. 9d. In Austria, we have smiths earning 4s. to 6s. a day; joiners, 5s. to 10s. a day; men employed in the building trades, about 2s. 8d.; and so on. Figures eloquent enough in themselves, but far more so when considered with relation to the value of money, and to the comfort and enjoyment for which they are exchangeable in Europe. In Wurtemberg, for instance, a single man can feed and lodge himself for from 10d. to 1s. a day. In Prussia, we find the various estimates of the annual charge of feeding a family of five persons varying in the several provinces between 11l. and 27l. a year. In Vienna, the working man's own estimate of living for a single man is put at 53l. 4s., including clothes and lodging; but it will be observed that the wages of that city are likewise very high.* The price of lodging for working-classes in Europe varies amazingly from year to year, and from place to place; generally speaking, however, the accommodation obtained will be both better and cheaper than in the cities of Brazil. Wages are not only at this high figure, but the upward tendency

* See Reports on condition of working classes presented to Parliament.

seems not yet to have exhausted itself; while the worth of the earnings is greatly enhanced by all kinds of associations, clubs, benefit and co-operative societies, which the emigrant must leave behind him.

But whatever be the cause, it is clear that the rate of wages in Brazil for skilled or heavy work is if anything *below* the best market price in the effete old world; while it is not to be presumed that the European would be wise in leaving country, associations, friends, language, customs and laws behind, to undertake an irksome journey, accustom himself to a depressing climate, risk a bout with yellow Jack or "febre perniciosa," overcome prejudices against him as an alien, perhaps as a heretic—in order, saddled with the cost of his journey, to begin a new life at the antipodes, even if, instead of something below or equal to his present earnings, he were quite certain of obtaining a good deal *more* than he had left behind. No snake would scratch off his old skin in the thorns, unless it were quite sure of the sleek splendour underneath. But besides the slavery of blacks, there exists a law in Brazil which creates something very like a slavery of whites. This is the law de locacaô dos serviços de estrangeros (a law respecting contracts for services of foreigners). Destined to place the foreigners entirely at the mercy of the natives, and calculated in many cases to reduce him to the position of a serf, this monster enactment is the product of the legislative genius and enlightened statesmanship of a nation that believes its future to be so linked with the successful introduction of foreigners, that it has not revolted from the most questionable devices in order to obtain them! It is, nevertheless, a characteristic issue of the lucubrations of a council of slave-holders. This law of October, 1839, establishes a monstrous inequality—first, between Brazilians and foreigners; secondly, between employer and employed, and is totally at variance with the general legislation of the empire, which (with certain usual exceptions) does not admit of imprisonment for debt. By its provisions, some of the results of which have already been seen in connection with the system of Parceria, any immigrant who has contracted to serve a native, say in repayment of the expenses of his passage out, or for advances made on his first helpless arrival, and who fails in his part of the contract, is liable, if he escape without "just grounds," to be seized in any part of the empire, and to be condemned to payment of the double amount of his debts to his employer, or in default to serve him for nothing for "the period wanting to fulfil the contract." Finally, he may be imprisoned, with or without hard labour, until he has paid the uttermost farthing, including the costs of the process, the extreme time of imprisonment being apparently limited to two years.* And the

* This is not very clear, as the qualifying clause occurs in a subsequent paragraph in which the case supposed is not identical.

application and interpretation of this law would be the affair of provincial magistrates such as those described in the following passage from a Report of Councillor Valdetaro, dated 1858 :—

"The justice of the peace and the referee appointed in the contracts do not offer the colonists a sufficient guarantee of impartiality and justice, especially in the case of those of different language, who have no connections in the country save with persons in a similar position to their own."

When we remember that some of the contracts made the head of the family responsible, not only for his own debts and those of his wife and children, but also for those of other so-called members of his family, and that the heir, contrary to all sane principles of law, the Roman included, was compelled to accept such a prejudicial inheritance, we have some idea of the bitter bondage thus created.*

Finding, then, race, religion, speech, customs, and laws alike unsuited to the English agricultural colonist, in what are we to seek a justification of his expatriation?

In the hospitable and admirable arrangements for the reception of emigrants; in the ease with which they find employment, through the assistance

---

* There were cases in the Metayer or Parceria colonies where debts of 1853 were not paid off in 1866, and those who ran away were imprisoned. Mr. Hermann Haupt says that in the majority of cases, when colonists under this system had succeeded in clearing themselves, it was in part owing to property left them in Europe.

of regular agencies giving honest information; in the facilities for the purchase of land, and for selection by means of maps of the required allotments; in the cheapness of that article; in security of title; in the favourable position of agriculture with regard to taxation; in the existence of good means of transport by land and sea; perhaps in the special openings for small industry here and there;—in all this, is there nothing that will serve our purpose?

Alas, I am afraid not. The reception of the emigrant, in spite of humane, enthusiastic impulses, is uncertain, his footing precarious. A refuge for immigrants was established under the auspices of the International Society of Immigration some years ago, but they were compelled, for want of funds, to make it over to the Government in October, 1866. During the time I was in Brazil —20 months—between 1869–71, there existed a similar establishment under the auspices of the Government; but I have known the food supplied there to be paid for by private benevolence of foreigners; and, on another occasion, in which many of my countrymen were concerned, the place had to be cleared by force, owing to a characteristic difference of opinion between the colonists and the Government as to who was responsible for their existence.

Such an institution as the Castle Gardens of New York does not exist, and this is the more to be regretted, that a night of exposure to torrential rains in the Campo de Santa Anna, as once happened to a body of British emigrants, or a delay of a few days on the sweet waters of the bay in the hot season, means, to a good many, fever and death. So many bad oranges in the case! Of the arrangements farther up the country, the progress of the Swiss to Nova Fribourgo, the preparations of Major Diaz at Rio Novo, and of latter years, Cananea, will give eloquent instances. I am convinced that all this will soon be, if it is not already, on a better footing, just as young niggers are better treated than ever of late; but our estimate cannot be formed on credit. The mere fact of so many emigrant vessels being brought to Rio at all, and that at times even in the hot season, shows with what carelessness the health of emigrants is exposed.

The same holds good of offices of labour such as so greatly facilitate the position of new-comers in the United States. They are either wanting, or have it not in their power to give the required information. With the exception of certain districts, Brazil is still, in spite of recommendations in laws of a quarter of a century ago, waiting for accurate maps and measurements of the disposable public lands; colonists have been kept waiting whole decades for their titles, and it has actually happened that the Government has sold lands which have afterwards been claimed by private persons.

Easy selection and acquisition, with sure title, are vital conditions of colonization, and Brazil would do well to study the arrangements to this effect in the northern half of the continent, where a new settler can, without leaving the port, pick out the exact locality and soil he prefers, with a certainty that he has not been overreached or deluded.

Nor, when all things are considered, can land in Brazil be called cheap. Formerly granted on leases, it is, since the laws of 1850 and 1854, only disposed of by sale. The lowest price is $\frac{1}{2}$ real a braça quadrada (6 feet square), or about $413\frac{1}{4}$ reis an acre (say 10d.); the highest, $1, 653 reis, as against from 10d. to 30s. in Canada, 1l. in Australia, 5s. in the United States. In the latter country, however, the laws of 1854 respecting gradual lowering of the price of unsold lands, reduces it, after thirty years without a purchaser, to $12\frac{1}{2}$ cents, about $\frac{1}{4}$ real a braça; while the Homestead Act of 1862 still further facilitates the acquisition of land, giving a certain acreage for a merely nominal consideration when cultivated for five years. Besides the price in Brazil, in the districts of colonies, is four or five times as much as the above maximum, reaching as high as 10 reals a braça quadrada, though the cost of measuring in that extravagant country has not been estimated higher than from 45 to 90 reals an acre. Under these circumstances, it is not astonishing to find that the average annual sale between 1859 and 1862 did not fetch more than from 2400*l.* to 2500*l.*, while it appears that Victoria effects yearly sales and leases to about 750,000*l.* a year, Tasmania to 87,000*l.*, New South Wales to 545,000*l.*, and the United States to the value of 1,000,000*l.*

While some of our colonies meet half their expenses with the profits of the sale and lease of public lands, Brazil also draws a large proportion of her income directly from the soil—*i. e.* no less than from 600,000*l.* to 800,000*l.* out of a revenue of 9½ millions from the coffee export duty alone. But it is not from the sale of waste and unprofitable territory, but from a direct burden upon agriculture, that this sum is obtained, nor does it include the "Pauta" or provincial dues, which in the province of Rio de Janeiro amount to nearly half as much again as those of the empire.* All this shows a considerable strain upon the goose with the golden eggs, that may eventually affect her laying.

With 4,891,394 square miles of territory, and only two inhabitants to each, we must not expect too much in the way of roads and lines of communication. In some provinces a good deal has been done and more projected; but, considering that this is a paramount object in the future of Brazil, the energy is not equal to the occasion. Several hundred miles of roads, equal to the finest

---

* That is the Pauta on coffee.

in the world, are to be found; but while in some cases there has been positive extravagance of imperial funds, the provincial high roads often remain in the state of miserable "picadas,"* or worse, as projects danced on the gusts of parish politics. What, however, especially concerns the colonist is the wretched state in which the colonial communication with ports and markets has in too many cases been allowed to remain. While new colonies are continually springing up, existing ones have been allowed to languish for want of proper connection with the outer world—and the complaints are very numerous on this score. It has been justly remarked that, had Brazil concentrated her efforts, the results would have been far more satisfactory. In 1856, no less a sum than 600,000*l*. was voted for purposes of colonization, and it has been estimated that of late years each emigrant cost from 10*l*. to 20*l*. Surely it were better to employ the greater part of these sums in opening up the country, thus rendering salaried puffing unnecessary, and leaving spontaneous emigration to do its own work. There is scarcely a question connected with the future of Brazil that does not halt and stick in the mud of the wretched "picadas," or in the thorns of the impassable "tacuadas."*

* Picadas are the tracks first hewn through the forest; tacuadas, matted jungle of the large bamboo.

Santa Viaria should have the fairest shrine in all the land, and every minister and public man bow down before her, and cry, "Roads, roads, roads!" Without veins blood cannot flow; and all galvanic tricks are empty folly.

The six existing lines of railroad are nothing to the requirements of the land. Though they are being extended, and others, such as that of Campos, Macahé, Sorocaba-Campinas, Jundiahy-Campinas, are projected, Brazil at present has but some 500 miles of iron way, while Switzerland has 2136, the United States 48,860! and British India, 4000!

With the coast communication, so important to some of the colonies, it was, a short time ago, no better, for though the road is in this case good enough, not everyone has the necessary capital to put a vehicle upon it. Sometimes steamers served certain places for a short time, and then were discontinued, to the infinite discomfort of those colonists who counted upon this mode of conveying their goods to market. The coasting trade was, until 1866, and may be again,* in the hands of natives alone, and the freights, in consequence of the monopoly, were often enormous. Mr. Tschudi mentions that on board a Brazilian ship a bale of

* Free permission to foreign vessels to ply in the coasting trade was extended to end of 1872. It has probably been again prolonged, but still only on short terms, and therefore the possibility of its being again withdrawn must be taken into our calculations.

cotton then cost more in going from Pernambuco to Rio than if sent from the latter place to Liverpool, and then back again on board a foreign vessel; also, that on one occasion the Government had to pay to a native ship five times the freight demanded for the same voyage by a foreigner—it being illegal to employ the latter! There are, moreover, but a limited number of ports with customhouses to which ships are allowed to trade. The navigation of the rivers is but feebly developed. There are several companies connected with the Amazons, one just started with emigration projects. There is a steamer or two on the San Francisco; the Bahia Steam Navigation Company; a small steamer on the Parahyba in communication with a monthly one from Rio to Campos—and there are a few plying at long intervals on some of the southern rivers. Projects in abundance spring up; now and then a new company appears or an old one collapses; but altogether there is no consolation to be sought in the steam navigation and river traffic, to console one for the want of railroads and highways.

The immense distances, bad roads, and want of steam or other public lines of transport form precisely one of the conditions which render the competition of the small farmer and lavrador so hopeless. In order to send his produce to the coast, the planter must possess a drove of mules in working order and be able to replace cripples. From ten to several hundred beasts will be required, according to the size of the estate; then there must be persons to look after them and cultivate grass for them, packsaddles, and all the rest. But, as this is far more than can be expected from many of the poorer agriculturists, they have to make arrangements with the nearest Fazendeiro possessing a drove of mules, in order to induce him to take down their coffee for them. This he is usually willing to do, and sometimes to buy it, of course on such terms as he considers favourable to himself; but, in the former case, he will naturally take down the whole of his own coffee first, and, by thus forestalling, obtain the best prices. In the distant competition in the port, it is clear that this is not the only point in which the small cultivator will come in weighted among the agents of rich planters. In almost every aspect of the financial question, from buying his slaves to bearing up against the sudden fluctuations of exchange,* though compelled to pay pauta and imperial taxes with the wealthiest, he will be at a great disadvantage. In preparing his produce it is the same. While the "café lavado" of the great Fazendeiro will have passed through seven or eight processes, until the grain comes out polished and tinted according to the last whimsical demands of fashion, the siteo's modest terredo will furnish

* These fluctuations ranged in 1868 from 1s. 2d. to 1s. 8d.

only roughly-shelled and discoloured berries, tainted with the harsh flavour of the mesocarp, and much less highly prized. The same remarks apply to the successful production of sugar for the market. We have seen how the lavradores of some northern provinces make use of the boilers and machinery of the Fazendeiro. Where this is not the case a settler without capital must always find it hard work to compete with the great slave-owning estates of the steaming lowlands. If small properties can ever compete effectually with large, which may sometimes very well be the case, it certainly is not where vast deserts interpose between the producer and the market, and slavery still further disturbs the natural conditions of the contest.

But there is yet another field left open to the small proprietor, the production of provisions— beans, maize, mandioca, potatoes, and vegetables, with, perhaps, an occasional pat of butter. It is the field of the Portuguese, who purchases a roça and first breaks ground for himself, and furnishes the principal means of existence in such starved colonies as Petropolis. No doubt, all these things can, with a little trouble, be produced in most parts of Brazil; and therefore it is certain enough that no man of the smallest energy and *knowledge of the country* need starve there *after the first six months*. But this, unless there be a large port or market within reasonable distance, is all; while colonists look, or ought to look, for something more. In the remote settlement, where no exchange can be effected with his surplus, the colonist must, at best, rest content with the plough-boy's ideal of a kingly life, "eat yourself full and then sleep." And when the food is farinaceous and the sleep lethargic, it must be a bad berth in the old world that the Saxon will not soon regret.

Where, then, are the exceptionable circumstances that justify the venture? If in nothing of all this, we can search no more, but only mutter—

"Que diable allait-il faire dans cette galère?"

Colonization in some form or other, ancient as the first movements of humanity, has in all ages been promoted by one of two considerations—either the welfare and advantage of the exile or of the land that sent him forth. The interest of the place of destination, of the spot selected, has, *with the colonist,* never been a motive. When, however, as sometimes happened, in Epidamnus and also in the Roman days for instance, wants of an old settlement have given the original impulse to a stream of emigration, the reinforcements thus invited, or the metropolis acting for them, took care to see that the interests of the emigrants fully coincided with those of the people requiring them. The community making the demand was, very properly, made to pay handsomely for what was so essential to its progress and existence, and this even to the amount of a third-part of the cultivated soil — the usual allotment to new settlers.

The world has seen many kinds of colonization, migrations by sea and land, for State ends or individual relief, as a result of hunger, of political oppression, or of ambitious enterprise; with a view to confirm and utilize conquest, or in order to advance and secure commerce. Now, the colonies were founded on known but little frequented districts among a sparse and semi-barbarous population, or in altogether virgin territories newly found and opened to the race; now they were planted in the midst of a vanquished civilization, or as armed piquets on the ancient march of commerce. But under all forms, from Naxos to Famagosta, from the days of Motya to those of Mexico, we find a leader of reputation, an organization on the home model, and such a connection with the mother-country as always secured moral sustenance, often vigorous material support. It is only in quite recent times that we first hear of the foundation of colonies in a heterogeneous medium, the oikistes being wanting, the metropolis ignored, and the organization matter of chance and speculation. Such settlements, left to the mercies of the inhabitants they come to reinforce, who, however enlightened and humane, behold the hazy interests of the new-comers only through the more monster mirage of their own—are veritable hen and duckling colonies. Within her sphere the mother's stout pinions would have afforded shelter and defence; beyond it, the pike may pick and choose *ad libitum*.

To spontaneous individual emigration distributing itself naturally over the land, by a skilful system of irrigation, flowing in obedience to law, in no matter how strong a stream, these remarks do not apply. But neither the diffusive agency, nor, except in certain German centres of the southern provinces, the attractive force exists in Brazil—while irregular enterprises under artificial stimulus are neither emigration nor colonization, but gross, and often reckless, importations of a delicate and perishable commodity. When, to continue the simile, Brazil shall have so trenched and prepared her fields, comprehended and applied the laws applicable to her case, cleansed and repaired the natural watercourses, the springs of the hills will of themselves descend and infuse fertility into the land by myriad rills, and when that day arrives there will be no longer need, either for pressure and inflated propaganda on the one side, nor for solemn warning on the other.

Distinguishing always, then, spontaneous individual emigration from mass emigration under pressure; and emphasizing once more the advantages derived by the latter form, which is that of true colonies, from metropolitan protection, with congenial organization and leadership—far be it from me to say that there is no opening for the Saxon under the Southern Cross, or to desire to taboo a liberal, orderly, and enthusiastic empire. Let intelligent, sober, industrious men, if possible, with a small sum of money in their pockets, go either to the healthy mining districts of Minas among their countrymen, or to the cool southern provinces, and if they are masters of some handicraft they have a fair chance of doing well; and, once started, may grow rich. But they will neither find diamonds in their drink-water nor gold-dust on their dirty boots, and will have to struggle against an alien speech, occasional prejudice, the competition of the cheap and nasty, bad, expensive lodging and clothing, and dear meat; while, if they be invested with the qualities presumed, they would have done as well elsewhere. Brazil, however, has, it must be admitted, that in common with most Transatlantic countries, that a keen, hard man of humble origin may, with luck, easier make a fortune there than in the old world; but it is a game which I would rather recommend to men from north of the Humber than to the ordinary southern Englishman. Quicksight in commerce, skill in mining and mechanics, soundness in finance, have filled, and will continue to fill, English pockets in Brazil. But men who thread such paths belong beyond the limits of this subject, and the question of labour importation. Still, as the good point of view of Brazil for Englishmen is in this direction, it is pleasant to advert to it. There are, then, many classes of workers, from bankers' clerks to Cornish miners, who have found good openings and done good business in the country, and a sojourn of ten or twelve years there, with intervals of absence, is, for a prudent, sober man, no more than an average price to pay for a competency.

The empire is orderly, secure, financially sound, fairly governed. Property is rarely attacked, blood never shed for pelf, no yearly revolutions occur, Gaucho brutality, Indian raids, and the horrible cry of "Muerte a los Estrangeros," is unknown.* The people, though sensitive, apprehensive, and jealous, are kindly, hospitable, inoffensive, and genial. They are ambitious of progress, intelligent, liberal, and though slow in executing, quick enough in comprehending new ideas. If we except manual labour, of which they have abhorrence, the Portuguese blood leaves with them, at least for some generations, an elastic spring of energy and a toughness of persistence not common in the tropics. As in most young States and young persons, there is much self-consciousness, often puerile self-satisfaction in the national sense; the desire of good govern-

* The rare, isolated, and feeble attacks of Indians, already mentioned, bear no comparison to the raids of the Plate districts.

ment, and especially of good reputation, being stronger than the habits of earnestness and abnegation necessary for their attainment. As in too many Catholic countries, public feeling in spiritual matters is, with certain numerically feeble exceptions, divided between apathetic indifference, sensual materialism, and gross superstition. While the newcomer must not expect to be treated as a native, nor to find in a young community either the reverent precedents or the good living he has left behind, he will encounter, with some wayward injustice not specially directed against him, many instances of a loyal desire to welcome him generously and treat him equitably, even though he be on the whole contemplated from an utilitarian point of view. But after the competency acquired, let him come home and marry in his own country.

I hope Brazil will give up *enticing* Englishmen. It can do her no good, and can do them harm. Persons of the class just alluded to, and the only ones suited on the whole to the country, will come without beckoning, and if these only stop twenty years, and then return like the Portuguese, Brazil will still obtain from them in this way not a little capital both of sinew and gold invested in her welfare. To be chary of English lives is quite compatible with the wish that they should be liberal with their money. Brazil wants the latter, and England has even more than is good. There is no need for her to quarrel with us because we will not lay our bones in her bosom. Let her take our gold and what we can give of energy instead. Though loth to supply her with labour, we have never stinted her in money, nor would we, seeing how punctually she pays. Let there, then, be no ill word between us because we are not anxious to replace her slaves, for is she not our foster-child? Were we not ally of her legitimate mother before ever she was born or thought of? Did not Cochrane, Earl of Dundonald, set her on her feet, establish her independence, deliver her from tutorship, drive off her enemies? Did not other Englishmen help teach her to walk? As she grew, did we not reprove her vices, and by an Aberdeen Act and a constant watch upon her coasts, compel her from her darling sin? Having purified her morals, did we not drain and cleanse her capital, help largely to construct her railways, roads, and docks, light her with gas and journalism, carry her correspondence, bank both with and for her, inundating her with sovereigns on her simple I.O.U.'s? Do we not take home her cotton, spin, weave, and return it to the value of over four millions sterling, while metamorphosizing sugar into iron, coffee into wool, linen, and sundries, to the value of some three millions more; taking, in a word, an approximate third of her exports in return for a similar proportion of imports supplied by us?

Let us, then, keep up this already pretty close connection, but beware lest it lead us beyond the bounds Platonic. Let us rejoice in the business ties that link us, and the solid profit we derive from one another. Let us endeavour to maintain intimate converse based on reciprocal advantage, the lively interest engendered by esteem; but let us revolt from combining to mix antagonistic breeds to the production of objects of mutual reproach and obloquy. Let us admire freely the soft Tupy, her feet in flowers, humming-birds and butterflies about her head; but let the admiration be seasoned with diffidence and chilled prudentially by worldly wisdom. In this manner we shall not be prone to slip from the safe footing of friendly intercourse and kindly offices, into the alluring blandishments of a connection that can only result in a projeny of Creole or even mongrel Britons, effete examples of parental folly.

The world is wide and varied, and somewhere, between the squat Lapp and giant Patagonian, must produce a race fitter than the British to live an agricultural existence in tropic South America, a people more sorely put to for a choice of habitation. May Brazil find and satisfy it. But before all things, she must begin by sweeping away the impediments and dispersing the phantom fogs that scare colonists from her shores. She must set to work to create a real attractive element within her boundaries, instead of wasting money and reputation on external propaganda, remembering that there is no harder trial of merit than empty eulogy and hyperbolical panegyric preceding trial. Though they may make dupes, they can never make friends; they may increase the appetite, but are sure to be followed by nausea and repugnance to simple food. The energies and funds hitherto squandered in driving in the guests should be expended in preparing the table, when, if the door be but left open, the savoury odour will itself be the most effectual advertisement, the solid fare the best gag on hostile criticism.

To name the most essential of these measures is to recapitulate the burden of this sketch. Climate and soil cannot be changed; but these shortcomings may be largely avoided by selecting for colonies good specimens of the latter, and ceasing to expose new-comers, through heedless selection of place and time of debarkation, and neglect of proper preparation, to all the ravages of the former. Ample and fitting accommodation, impartial agencies, bureaux of information, accurate demarkation of land, and secure title at lower prices than the present —facilities of transit to the various sites of saleable territory, and development of their means of communication by construction of roads and establishment of regular lines of steam communication, whether by land, river, or sea—all this, together with good maps and pamphlets, containing sound and simple information, void of all splendid mendacity, will enable the Government to dispense with much embarrassing interference in emigration matters. The only European agencies allowed should be the consulates, who might give as much curt information, while assuming as little responsibility, as possible. The very fact that a foreign Government is answerable for his destiny saps the best energies and paralyzes the self-reliance of the emigrant. If a bridge existed between Cape Frio and Cape Roca, half the anxious problem would be solved. Men would wander into the Western land on their own responsibility; those who liked the look of it would remain, those who did not would, when they could, return, without a right to cast the blame of their failure on anyone but themselves. The presence, moreover, of this feeling with them would often conjure of itself all chance of failure from their path. Let Brazilians build such a bridge, if not literally, by the best substitute possible, subsidies to steamers in order to *cheapen passages to Brazil*. Let a certificate from the consulate suffice, without too close an examination, to obtain still further assisted passages, and let them rather be given freely to persons of all useful classes proposing to stay over five years in Brazil, than fixed at a very low rate. Independent of this, let everything be done to reduce the cost of the voyage to Brazil—to build, in fact, the bridge.

The present race of Brazilians have received the hideous polypus growth of slavery from their fathers: they are aware of the danger from loss of blood in too sudden amputation. They must, however, also remember, that there is as much risk of anœmia or chronic deterioration of the circulating fluid, where the cure is spread over too long a period. The ligature already applied by the late emancipatory measures must be drawn tighter and tighter by a fearless hand, for only when the fungus shall fall severed to the ground will it be possible for the body politic to assume a healthy condition, and for the pure current of free and honourable labour to circle in its veins. A high, and perhaps progressive, tax upon all city slaves—originally, I believe, an idea of Count Jequetinonha—would be a judicious pull at the ligature.

As agriculture will have to bear the shock of this great change, so it is the more essential that it should be freed from a portion at least of the vast share which is allotted it of the burdens of the State. In any country the source of wealth must be the source of revenue; but there are other branches of trade and industry, other fields in which considerable fortunes are now made, on which it would not seem unreasonable to throw, at least for a time, a larger portion of the charges pressing so heavily on the indebted Fazendeiro and his caffetal. Such a policy would be perfectly consistent with a tax on land, especially if calculated in inverse ratio to its cultivation. It is the *dead hand* from which the gold must be squeezed, leaving the living one as free as can be for the work of life.

If there are some weighty laws peculiarly obnoxious to the emigrant, especially the northern emigrant, they are not many. In general, it is rather with the administration of the codes than with their context that there is room for much amelioration. In such an empire, of nearly 5,000,000 square miles, and an independent existence of only half a century, some weakness and corruption in the extremities, some sacrifice of the principle to the person in remote provinces, is inevitable; and those who consider the blind and bloody codes of a century ago in Europe; the evasions and arbitrary perversions of justice even now practised in that venerable quarter of the world, will not haste to throw stones. But when we come to find just causes of complaint, such, for instance, as the long delays consequent on insufficient provisions for bringing prisoners rapidly to trial, in the *very capital*, one of the most busy emporiums in the world, the case is quite otherwise.

That the peculiar laws of succession to property, especially in the matter of division, and in the effects of marriage without contract, are prejudicial to many colonists, and sometimes take them painfully by surprise, there can be little doubt; but it must be left to Brazilian statesmen alone to consider whether a compulsory division between the children be altogether as likely as free testamentary disposition to encourage in a young community the full improvement and development of landed estates.

Legislation with a view to the complete dissipation of all shades of social or political inequality or distinction connected with religious differences, is highly essential, and especially the speedy introduction of *bonâ fide* civil marriage, unhampered by saving clauses, and accompanied by facilities for the due celebration and registration of the same. The substitution of the monstrous labour law of 1839, by legislation showing a sincere desire to defend and protect the immigrant from all the harpies who may desire to prey upon him, and from the imposition to which he is exposed on first arrival in a foreign land; the reform of the present militia organization and system of recruiting for the army, rendering it impossible to pervert either into instruments of political tyranny and of petty local persecution; the more perfect control and moderation of the autocratic influence of the legion of delegados and petty police officials; measures calculated to ensure the integrity and high character of the magistracy (juizes de paz and juizes de orfaôs), as also the morality and intelligent devotion of the clergy; the establishment of a sufficiency of schools and churches;—in fine, all and any enactments tending, by decentralization, to the quickening of local life, to the extirpation of the political weed which has overrun all domains of national economy, and to the development in its place of a vigorous communal and municipal growth, in which foreigners should be admitted to a full participation both in council and fruition—all this would indicate the inauguration of a policy likely to do more to benefit and secure the future prosperity and increase of the empire, than many gallons of ink expended in vapid propaganda, or acres of surface covered with the rosiest placards.

But though in this way Brazil may become esteemed and respected, and her people multiply and replenish her wildernesses, the calling and natural field for the English working-man lies, let it well be understood, elsewhere. Not being Hobson, he need not take Hobson's choice. Indeed, such has hitherto so invariably been the fate of the white man in the drowsy woods of tropical America, that I believe the Briton would be really happier, and truly in more congenial circumstances, under the perpetual scud and drizzle of the bleak Falklands, than amid the enervating glories of a South American jungle.

But, after all, the Falkland Islands are not the only British settlements, not to mention kindred lands, open to the emigrant. Besides an absorption of some 200,000 per annum by the United States, Canada can, it would appear by the last Commissioner's Report, absorb from 30,000 to 40,000 a year.

Australia, New Zealand, and other colonies require Englishmen. Queensland is even ready to give gratuitous passages for certain classes. Both the United States and the Canadian Pacific Railroad schemes will give unusual advantages to emigrants selecting allotments on their route. Pine-clad Vancouver's is a queen of islands. The Cape has finer diamonds than Minas; and for those that *will* sit under palms at any price, is there not the gorgeous archipelago of the West Indies, where one jewel sleeps in the shadow of another? Surely it were as well to help indigent and wandering Englishmen to these shores, as to expend equal sums in bringing Coolies from the far-off East. For those who have a little money or education there are territories occupied by the Anglo-Saxon race where money gives 20 per cent. interest; and districts, such as the valleys of California, where the fertility of the soil is only surpassed by the almost frenzied activity of the neighbouring ports.

But this glimpse of Saxon colonization prospects in Brazil is no place for a catalogue of the colonies and settlements of British race. A good wine needs no bush; and the forlorn fatuity which has guided Englishmen to the sign of the Palm and Golden Apples, can alone excuse John Bull from this once hanging out a little one.

www.ingramcontent.com/pod-product-compliance
Lightning Source LLC
Chambersburg PA
CBHW020103170426
43199CB00009B/374